Muybridge's Horse

Muybridge's Horse

a poem in three phases

Rob Winger

NIGHTWOOD EDITIONS
Gibsons Landing, BC

Published by Nightwood Editions, 773 Cascade Crescent, Gibsons, BC, Canada V0N 1V9 www.nightwoodeditions.com

Edited by Silas White. Cover design by Carleton Wilson. Author photo by Kristal Davis. Printed and bound in Canada.

Nightwood Editions acknowledges financial support from the Government of Canada through the Canada Council for the Arts and the Book Publishing Industry Development Program (BPIDP), and from the Province of British Columbia through the British Columbia Arts Council, for its publishing activities.

 Canada Council for the Arts    BRITISH COLUMBIA ARTS COUNCIL
Supported by the Province of British Columbia

This work combines elements of biography and invention, including quotations from both scholarly and historical sources to involve it in an ongoing conversation. Characters, dates, locales, geographies and narratives have been altered or embellished, in some cases, to spin the right kind of yarn (a racetrack shifted six years into the historical future, a character or two emerging out of hearsay). But, the essential story and emotion of the work remains true to recorded historical experience, despite rearrangements of chronology and resituations of the factual archive.

Library and Archives Canada Cataloguing in Publication

Winger, Robert, 1974–
     Muybridge's horse / Rob Winger.

A poem.
ISBN 978-0-88971-231-7

1. Muybridge, Eadweard, 1830-1904—Poetry. 2. Photographers—United States—Poetry. 3. Photographers—United States—Biography. I. Title.

PS8645.I573M89 2007   C811'.6   C2007-901474-7

He is dead and he is going to die....
Whether or not the subject is already dead,
every photograph is this catastrophe.

−Roland Barthes

The first sentence of every novel should be:
"Trust me, this will take time but there is order here,
very faint, very human."
Meander if you want to get to town.

−Michael Ondaatje

Today everything exists to end in a photograph.

−Susan Sontag

Contents

Prologue

1. OCCIDENT

2 3 4 5 6 7 8 9 10

Copyright 1878 by MUYBRIDGE

MUYBRIDGE'S HORSE

the second in walking when both of your feet are airborne

the time between target and gunshot

water in your throat

the space of decline when a masseuse's thumb slips
    from a knotted muscle

the position between balance and impact with the earth

my fingers submerged in ocean, in a dive

the moment, in a train lavatory,
    when a sideways sway throws a spray of urine
    away from the bowl's mouth

any sporting ball suspended

the heat of tongues before lips contact

the time between an engine and the sound of it

the stretching of a knuckle before it cracks

a drill changing its tonality as it contacts a sheet of maple

whole snowflakes as they meet your mouth

a minute hand jumping to its next hour before the clock can chime

the stretched pressure of a guitar string before sound

the darkness that happens before any object collides with your face

the second of ease when the piano you're pushing has built up
    enough force   to glide

any form of jumping

waves

a bird in flight

Beans

At the Bradley and Rulofson galleries in 1873, Eadweard grips a coffee mug in a palm weathered by collodion. He holds his arm out forty-five degrees from the shoulder, extends a hand's pocket into your foreground. He's burnt a decade of darkroom acids into these lifelines, and the skin flakes off after baths or sunburns. Fingers choreographed around pottery, layers let loose in every kind of water. He doesn't take a good photograph until he's thirty years old. Like me.

The Guatemalan beans in his cup were pulverized down the street, Folger's leaking their aroma into the San Francisco sunshine each morning. Eadweard opens the shop door with one precise swivel of elbow, strides into the room on time, winding flawlessly around wares, towards the marble counter, holding a tripod under a bicep. He always pays in exact change, lifts the warmth of brews to his mouth, tips the brow of his hat, pivots towards the door, completing, and steps into light. Without language. His beard, then, before the Napa county jail cell, still a velvet shock of black against the suit collars, still spilling confidently in front of where a necktie might have been.

Today's steam from the cup lifts past Eadweard's lips, past his slate-grey eyes, past three miniature ocean views on the walls of the gallery, facing West.

This is before the earthquake.

Before Flora, Floredo, Harry Larkyns. Before Leland Stanford's horse lifts its four forelocks in a singular suspension of chemistry. Before a succession of bodies crowds his lenses with the insistence of American bone, dry negatives erasing three decades of recipes with their manufactured balances of development. Before the Plaza of Antigua, the stream at San Isidro, the patchwork view from Nob Hill, redefine Eadweard's understandings of time. Before and after England. Long before Eadweard invents motion pictures in a makeshift shed on the Palo Alto stock farm, everything we knew about movement changed by a single animal's inertia.

Versions of a coastline.

POCKETS

He almost always wore a hat.

He ate raw lemons,
kept in the enormous inside pockets of suit jackets,
bitten to stay alert,
composed.

He refused to wear shoes with laces.

He feared umbrellas,
thinking their ribs would collapse on him.

He kept a snapshot of Flora,
his wife, cornered
in his left trouser pocket,
against the thigh.

The watch in his vest's right pocket
wound at 8 a.m. each morning,
placed on top of the lungs.

When focusing, framing,
he tucked the tip of his beard
into white chest pockets.

While trekking up mountains,
he was fond of hiding
specialized equipment
between his pants' waistlines
and the small of his back,
properly hidden under wool
and enormous backpacks,
layers against a faded hillscape.

We never get to know him.

Part One: Flora

Muybridge on "Contemplation Rock, Glacier Point."
Yosemite Valley, 1872. Uncut stereoscopic print.

[Western]

ALBUM I:

POSSIBLE
ROUTES

Liquid Light

1.
in their opaque tents,
the earliest photographers are necessary chemists

they dip coated windows into silver nitrate
until they turn creamy yellow

as the emulsions dry, they lose sensitivity
negative carriers dripping trails onto dirt

from bath to camera
where operators cram glass into their careful envelopes of air

because the lens cap hasn't been invented,
they cover their apertures with hats

     six seconds of light before ripping the pictures free

2.
like Eadweard, collodion is born in England
and migrates

     a chemical compound first used to dress wounds,
     it's originally a varied mixture of gun cotton, alcohol, and ether
     that fuses into gummy liquid over open military sores

when its photosensitivity is discovered,
it disinherits hospitals
to dress glass negatives with blood memories

     three hundred times less sensitive than twentieth-century film

3.
in his early darkrooms, Eadweard births outlines

he pours pyrogallic acid over latency,
lets cyanide neutralize pregnancy,
development finally destroyed by his water baths.

this way, Eadweard ends every image with dryness

trusts liquid in the present tense and then
eliminates it

FIXING THE RIVER

Eadweard's maternal grandfather dealt in pigeons
filled their silver chests with folded messages
relied on wind, releasing
    so hired dock hands downriver
    mistook every shadow for a bird

this grandfather's virtuous wife outlives him
with nine children
teaches, stews, scrubs,
orders men to fill Atlantic ships with old-world minerals
to float across the water

each transaction stiffening her towards a certain

    photograph
    where her face droops awkwardly,
    unsmiling
    lips unwanted bolts in the steel casting of clothing

    she teaches Eadweard *only thieves and rascals are afraid*
    forces him to make mince pies for neighbours at Christmas time
    says *hold up your head and speak out*

    in the portrait,
    she is about to rise
    frustrated with each moment that the operator
    prepared chemistry,
    positioned perspective,
    this bulge in the stiff fabric that is her impatient knee, ready

    she dies in 1870, four years before her daughter does
    Eadweard watching them both get buried,
    seeds.

Susannah, Muybridge's mother, is gentler
she sees two of her four sons die,
collapses inward,
washes memories of her men in acids
that fog their outlines

she grows old in Kingston-upon-Thames
with Eadweard's only surviving brother,
who crowds their house with clocks
daily opening their bellies to gears, switches, ticks
attempting,
as a minor hobby
to have them *all strike at exactly the same moment*

    here, she grows wary of burglars
    positions dozens of fedoras at the front door
    a silver teapot on the stairwell,
    hoping
    any criminal would see the hats,
    assume a high male population,
    take the teapot
    and run
    from her conspiracy of watches

when she dies, on the hour, in 1874, the house explodes in bells

by then,
Eadweard is growing
famous in California for shooting scenes
and people:
    Harry Larkyns,
    Leland Stanford
    Flora Shallcross Stone
    Floredo Helios Muybridge
    Occident

Seward's Folly, Farallone Islands,
Antigua, Nanaimo, Alcatraz,
San Francisco, Sacramento, Portland,
London, New York City

Yosemite Valley and environs
Cathedral Rock, Mammoth Trees,
Woodward's Gardens, Mount Watkins in mist

all stopped rivers
in the camera's fluid frames

Overland Express, or, the Birth of Helios

1.
This is how lawyers and biographers use desert
to stage Eadweard's abandonment of language
for animals and cameras,

how responsible versions name his first horses as the mustangs
shouldering the Butterfield mail coach through a sliver of desert,
detailing how
they scythe a path east, towards imagery,
take the shortest, most difficult route from the Golden State
attempting to unfurl America from the inside out
  the heroics of discovery

This is how the driver loses control,
cabin's pitch and roll,
passengers clutching embroidered ropes
with each swell of hooves
how
   one rider, delirious, leaps into air
   his skull leaking into the blackfly sand where he lands

When the story's reins finally slip free,
Eadweard's beard emerges from carriage
to oxidize in desert air,
flat form knifed across landscape

the boulder his head finds
bookends him in air

when he turns,
the hot sky flips over on its back

2.
This is how he wakes up cordially,
sees two carriage wrecks with slight alterations in perspective

sliding across sand
he watches renditions of his horse overlap

the carriage's oak shell, crumpled, doubles
careful animal's dusty breath rising in two folds

how every image displays its twin:

> birth of stereoscope

3.
This is how they find him,
an overexposed halftone
> the blonde curls in his mind
> translated into shades
> all his locks pressed grey in the sunwaves' weight

the boulder that shuttered him
is a stitch of time,
shows him what locomotion means

This is how he exits the air, officially, on a stretcher
every outline suggesting second possibilities:

> a horse; a mustang
> a split carriage; a mail car
> double curvature of *the sangre de cristo*

carried to the ambulance car,
red pooling in his temples,
he memorizes the space between realities

> thinking names

4.

later, in the hospital,
he will claim the loss of taste,
smell

   will reduce himself to simple geographies
   test his double visions with a spoon that inverts
   his bandaged forehead into an ivory ship

   he will carry the spoon's hollow
   from one soup bowl to his palate,
   and replace it in the other soup bowl's emptiness

      suturing edges

SAN FRANCISCO CAMERA

1.
for a full picture, we need minor
characters,
to sketch typical masters.

we need to specify how
it's before the accident, on Montgomery Street,
1860s America,
that Eadweard meets social Silas Selleck,
daguerréotyper

> a man whose moustache
> completely hid his upper lip in white whiskers
> entire mouth disappearing when he grinned

we need chronology,
so that when Eadweard arrives in San Francisco
selling classical British fiction,
Silas is there,
hiring,
how

> he slaps a dripping plate into Eadweard's hands
> says, *Put this in the pyro, will'ya?*
>> *Got a lassie up yonder won't wait another minute!*

> disappears out the door,
> Eadweard's sealed suitcases heaped in an entranceway

we need records for how
he teaches Eadweard to see the world
in frames
to look at the most casual scene in terms of
exposure

> city, translated:
> light-tight architecture

2.

this is specific history, then.

living here means
people are still shot for looking at certain men
with the wrong angles in their mouths

that's why Silas scoops Eadweard out of continental manners
submerges his burning cuticles in certain acids
says, *this is American nitrate*
    this instrument, made to polish surfaces

why Eadweard moves his hands across focal planes
    to the edges of things
unhinges his jaw and jams its shutter with cigars

why Silas takes him into bars and fills him with beer
    this is what it means to succeed
    leans in,
    the moustache over the pint
    or lose

3.

this way, at the start of things,
Muybridge first pushes into the Yosemite Valley
soaked in San Francisco iodide
slips acidic kneecaps into carriers
sun solidifying joints

he scratches "Helios" into his first stills
wanting that identity felt,
blood scooped from his back

Silas there handing out recipes:
    how to get to Santa Barbara
    how to shoe a horse

the measured bath of uncharted waterfalls
hardens him
so that, re-entering architecture,
Eadweard's a logical negative
slips into Selleck's studio
grey whiskers against white trim,

    clocked

4.
the picture as public record, then.
as verb.

the picture as a hot line of words
spit out the nickel mouth of a private press.

the revolution of ink that means
poem,

that is edition. the opinion in a paper's
grain.

5.
a year (or a century) later,
at the North Point dock,
Eadweard shapes an O
with his forearms
rests its oval on his knee
cradling the harbour's lip

      in the print
      the ship's chain is attached to his torso
      links receding to a plump hull,
      tapering diagonally into distance

      his face is lit only by the speckle of sun on his nose
      hat's brim blackening features
      hot heart gone iron
      in noon sea salt

      the masts are skeletons

      in the print,
      the sea is so pale that ships levitate
      Muybridge, chained to their bones,
      solid black,

      anchoring

the chain, umbilical
hull to throat,
its oxygen circulating through
the truth in negatives

body a blood clot in the metal's flow

Photograph of Eadweard Pretending to Slip from a Yosemite Valley Mountain

1.
he reads the map with complete faith,
wedges himself into scenery as though plunging into water
lenses wrapped in cloth,
aimed at stratosphere

on his back,
saddled
a portable eighty-pound darkroom,
    wet plates flattened against shoulder blades
    threatening them
    with a geography of scratches

he looks into the air and sees borders

2.
arriving in the Upper Montane zone of the Sierras,
Eadweard must have sweated alone through two distinct timberlines,
abandoned groves of ponderosa pine and incense cedar
flanked by unrecorded Douglas fir

he must have passed a three-hundred-foot Sequoia
that's later named the largest living thing on earth
trunk and crown the width of a street or house
    52,599 cubic feet of wood
    ten times heavier than the largest whale

this is long before
the biggest specimens here are named and measured
by governments and tourists
out of respect for survival and fire scars

Eadweard pacing this alphabet of grain

3.
It's at a cliff's granite brim
that he stops, folds his map
sits on a boulder, measuring red firs, Jeffery pines,
watching the scene for several minutes, still

when the stereoscopes emerge, their sides pivot into chambers
he inserts stops, slowly adjusts cartography

    the inventory of privacy

pulls lenses from his back as though removing muscles

    his pack, the frames in his head

        walks to his foreground's margin, arranging the dirt there

           takes a lemon from his pocket and bites

               grey twist of beard outlining the anonymous forest

4.
Eadweard most likely inserts the camera into glacial ice,
pulls an emulsion from its hollow
like a letter from an envelope

acid dripping from the machine's back,
he thinks numbers, sunspots,
constructs negative limits

as he wedges an ice pick's toenail into mountain,
    strings his body from it,
    an arrow in a taut bow,
    Nevada Falls, vertical,
    in the background,
    imitating,

he gives us the rare grin that becomes this picture

facing tripod, then,
exposing valley,
he must have pulled a tied cloth from the lens
with a rope
strung
from camera to body

    before freezing
    in respect for chemistry

returning to the metal eye,
covering it,
this is how
Eadweard would have exploded
in adjectives,
leapt into air,

    not joy, but a mirror of scenery

    this picture

    the body reflecting
    the body reflecting the earth
            reflecting the body

Blossom Rock

1.
from letters, we know that Eadweard is always aware of water

when he enters it in December of 1869
beneath the waters of the Bay,
a considered glass sphere encloses the camera
in a see-through sack

men slip from ships
opening the blue surface

they carry nitroglycerine vials to the face
of Blossom Rock, on the bottom,
chip trenches into granite
with knives
slipping explosions into possibilities,
ordering migrations

    the divers emerge holding fuses
    lines from the ships to the Rock to the bodies
    a contour drawing

    haul themselves from liquid

Muybridge works himself frantic
    slips acids into the sack's dry globe
    seals the stiff lung closed,
    and drops the ball back into ocean,
    angry at motion

he plunges his face into blue,
    salt stinging his pupils so drops fall out
    invisibly,
    into sea

he pulls the orb from the bay
    scales skin,
    removes vital organs to a bucket
    replaces bait with a new glass plate,
      repeats, repeats, repeats

      arms braced against the circular sunlight

2.
when the other ships drift away for the explosions,
Muybridge stays

he drops a dozen negatives into the swells
wet whiskers leaking from his chin like blood

    he confuses the water with sky,
    lifting his head

    looking for oxygen

3.
on paper,
the only evidence of illumination
comes with a wipe of whiteness
as the boat
is lifted out of liquid,
camera bag hanging in the air:
    an uprooted bulb

he preserves
then hides
these failed records
recalling salt,
the shapes in waves,
how to record such privacies
without overexposure

rock's pale violence
losing its borders
in all that abstract glass

COAST

1.

when the Yosemite exposures win awards
Eadweard's bank account fattens

he boards iron
studying US military coasts,
makes moving positives of Seward's Folly
to subdue the angry imagination of Americans

the beauty of edges turning over in his brain
as he charts continental limits
all the way north

defining shoreline

2.

he politely poses actors
to simulate the Modoc war
to stage the last proudly official slaughter
of nations
in manifest destiny
to sell viewcards as parlour tricks

he cuts moon holes into glass
so that flawless lunar circles float over every beach,

splices cloud studies together with hour-long evening landscapes
two negatives on each image, c-section horizons

one half of his vision in every fiction:

Camera Lucida

ALBUM II:

FLORA
SHALLCROSS
STONE
MUYBRIDGE

1.
my name was labelled
by American men
thinking of nothing
but motion

so, when I die
(at the end of the poem)
at twenty-four,
whole calendars are covered
with each man's
gravity

2.
Eadweard's elbows were shaped
just like the porch swing
that my father, Mr. Shallcross,
built
and set me in,
a toddler,
blue bonnet framing my pink puckered cheeks

     its arc tilting the horizon:
     my first memory of men

father chose my name himself,
said he wanted me to be roses

     chrysanthemum syllables falling
     against my infant skull,
     pollen infiltrating the house,
     feeling its way from the proper sitting room
     to the kitchen
     where my mother was,
     spread-eagled in afterbirth,
     on the table, dying

     she wanted me named *Mercy*

when she goes,
our birth and death certificates get
confused:
she takes my name,
buries it

     half of me gone before beginning

3.
the first time I get married I'm sixteen,
having left the South for California gold,
     father dying on a Mississippi evening
     in his swing

Mr. Stone stopped that movement
by taking me to bed,
after church,
changing my name,
officially
     his rhythm on top of me
     a second version of my father's hammer

     I closed my eyes and prayed for angles

Mr. Stone was the best-named man I ever met
everything about him was granite
the few words he dropped towards me,
sweating in the kitchen of his dreams
blocked all the pathways in the house
with boulders

     I approached every room,
     in those days,
     dodging avalanches

I learned to paint prints
because Mr. Stone wanted the world permanent
took the brush and
glossed realities
self-employed,
moving negatives

      I learned about incident, focus
      the depth of field in a man's vision

      I erased cedars
      powdered women's faces with kind glazes
      darkened the crotches of men with egos

      every finishing touch a kind of naming

4.
when I met Eadweard, wet brush in hand,
I'd never seen anyone move in such careful lines
      each rotation of wrists,
      considered

      he came into rooms in spotless raking diagonals
      found his targets and went straight for them,
      careful beard shaped just like a cataract's gravity

that afternoon,
he introduced himself with imagery
      presented views of the Sierra Nevada,
         tiny figures on continental Cathedral Rock
      criticized the smallest fog as though
      blemishes on skin
all this, without language
the patient tilt of his palms

How did you get to all these places?

still serious,
he unlatched a rosewood case,
loosened brass knobs from a finely crafted mounting
    slid a picture directly into my hand
    in one continuous gesture

    This, he said, taking my nails, touching them to glass
    Helios, flying studio.

in my hand:
    an outdoor darkroom scattered across hillside
    bottles flowering foreground
    the dark aperture of a cave where an ebony tent is set
    hat sitting on a stone's stomach

he brushed my wrist, requesting return
    rough knuckles
waited for me, staring

    Flora Stone, I said
    and he snapped his studio back into its case

    left the room with superlative geometry

    I entered his photos as though stepping into maps

5.
proposal

Eadweard stands, three months later
carefully composed in the oak doorway
a logical bouquet of roses,
intentional, red
in his tight hand
spines pinching fingerprints

      when I put his palm to my breast
      the blood cupped there leaves a nipple on the lace

      I lead his hands, spoon them into me
      calluses brushing bare shoulders

when I pivot his limbs,
cords rise to meet my hollows
Eadweard, still,
allows me to direct him
watches his elevated arm,
      follows the sierra flames of my hair
      to the November lips
      that taste his digits there

        my talcum clouds his face
        and I watch him inhale me,
        smell hidden sweat
        nose expanding with pollen,
        so he hardens
        realistic,
        memorizing my curves,
        measuring

when I orbit him,
he stays wooden,
placed

the slow pivot of my pelvis against him,
his arm in the air where I've left it

    his beard falls across my face and I take bits of it into my mouth

    my hot, deliberate tongue across his neck
    is the only language we have to conjugate

6.
that night,
a midnight chill
fogs the rims of objects

kitchen tables float out of the sea of it
the prows of naked ships
soft riptide of my walking,
such cautious floating,
floor

as I fumble for a doorknob's egg
feet on cold tile
    I see my breath
    in a Shakespearean crack of moonlight

        clock ticking
        beads of rain
        in the cool width of the bedroom

his body roped to the bed

        anchor line

                hull

           heart

7.
when we marry,
he channels four solitary decades
into my twenty-two grounded years
and I love the water in him

at first, you see,
Eadweard lacks all architecture
offers me currents and fiction

we decorate our apartment
with pictures of clouds
and
for two years
all the windows on the wall
are possibilities for flight

8.
desert honeymoon

we watch mountains fold the sky into place
hills kneading storm clouds,
the sun's heat, rising

(in the Sierra Nevada,
 we sleep in a cemetery of wood)

this room's skin,
lined in oak, lodgepole pine,
spruce, Douglas fir, maple:
tree grains sealing us into blue
prints,

the nails in the floor are birthmarks

by nightfall, the orange ceiling sings

fireplace flames
lick us with careful heat,
paint brief walls

we both understand that
in the morning
the air will be cold, again

Eadweard will trace its trajectory
through the throat,
past grizzled bristles
over this neck's crescent
that holds the sunlight,
like the room did
and into the lungs' quick heat,
cold fire
steam lifting from lips
to the back's range

we untie the landscape
like a hand would

9.
later
he leaves me alone in San Francisco
for six months at a time
chasing shadows with used chemistry

while he walks Yosemite rivers
I go through his vistas
violating water
wanting him slowed, continual

I blur the streams

the day he comes back,
he hardly notices the inertia I've altered,
says nothing

when I try to coax him to the bedroom,
cotton dress slipping from collarbones
he remains,
fixed
     on the wingback chair
     staring at the wall

when I ask him what he sees
in the square angles of the ceiling
he says,
carefully

   the square angles of the ceiling

(dress frozen on the floor,
 winter)

10.
that night,
with whisky in him
Eadweard goes precisely abstract
gulps amber and loses generalities,
bottle's clarity dividing dusk against the wall

he approaches me holding the shot glass
puts its coldness against my cheek,
watching
takes my right arm, raises it above my head
crooking the elbow,
so my forearm lifts like a teapot's spout
sets one finger to my chin,
its weight on my lip

he disappears, for a moment, into our tiny, crowded study
that always smells of mothballs

returns with a brown roll of paper

the map uncurls against the wall,
Eadweard holding its top above me
paper brushing my back as it flattens out
West Coast echoing my figure:

the armpit, British Columbia
the hips are San Francisco
my middle's curve
        the heat in Panama

he rolls the glass over my hips
and a hammer tacks the continent
against wallpaper
in two quick drumbeats

he puts the shot to his lips:

Flora.

holds me against the bottle's emptiness

my body, a shore

11.

Daily Alta California. July 19. 1875: "Poor Flora is a-cold"

two years later,
paralyzed
I decide to die

    (Eadweard run away
    to be with his ghosts and inertia)

I become sundial,
lie silently crisp in my hospital bed
for two intentional weeks,
allow nurses to raise arms,
    spin my waist for sponging,
    hold my dormancy in their busy palms, dead fish

I give the woman holding my hand
some final language, sentiment
    I am sorry
    and it washes over her,
    a burst cloud

I swallow only fluids,
block pollen from the mind,
concentrate on stillness

a deliberate slope of stars
staged
in the window pane

morning slanting across the white walls in yellow pyramids

    the only language I want to happen here
    finally,
    thinking of earth:

    Mercy

ALBUM III:

HARRY

SELF-PORTRAIT AS A SEA BIRD

1.

>my name is Harry Larkyns
>(*Bonjour, je m'appelle Harry*)
>(*Ola. Harry Larkyns, matador!*)
>this is what I've seen:

I've tasted, deliciously, the breasts
on three continents of women
uncurled bodice strings, unstrung milk
siphoned the colours of creamy pocketbooks
into me. (*Oui, merci!*)

>my shaded jawline
>rests profoundly on crisp collars.

>it holds my minty teeth (which I polish nightly, practising French)
>around consummate lips,

>my neatly flattened sideburns
>soften the black orbits of my eyes

>my suits are wings

in London, I progressed from a coal-pit poverty of youth
into a fiction of abandonment:

>my family disowned me, nobly,
>as I plunged into high-class theatre
>where sensible riches wouldn't follow me into drama

>in ethical desperation, I enlisted,
>became a heroic actor in the Punjab

>polishing pistols, still handsome, I won striped war decorations
>and earned the right to robe myself in Indian saffron

escaped to the Turks' legal brothels, then, the story goes,
returned to London, a Nabob, a caged bird

I joined the French army as a hero, and returned, Romantic,
to London, where Wordsworth was dying

perched myself at the edge of the island,
waiting for the right wind

2.
arriving in America,
I pried apart Eastern cities like the legs of prostitutes

I became a social businessman, a white-horse hero

I targeted the epicentres of Yankee socials
and stopped dances with my footwork
punctured crowds, smelled their energies, inhaled

audiences saw themselves in my soliloquies, and loved me for it

I gave them my versions of India-France-England,
and they paid me in women

I worked at circuses, mines, newspapers, theatres

I scripted entrances, swooped into scenes on invisible strings,
the magic of flight

3.
I first approached San Francisco in '72 with a portable purse
    named Arthur Neil

he paid for everything, convinced that 1000 pounds was waiting for me
(he believed in me because my accent spells refinement)

in November, released from desert,
we checked into the Occidental Hotel
where relief comes in the form of free
whisky and petite chamber maids

I downed the bottle's fire and ordered
Atlantic lobster cracked open on a Pacific budget,
copper heat boiling my guts as I invited the girls to join us

I slapped Neil's back, dumped poison down his throat

>   hot friction of the women
>   against the cool certainty of finance

I insisted we tip at every opportunity,
dropped jewels into the women's brassieres that they spooned away
into the secrecy of corsets
their bodies, mining sites

4.
when Neil unfolded his plans for Honolulu,
I straightened them
made myself,
for all intents and purposes,

>   *anecessaryconsultantforbusinessaffairs*
what with
>   *myexpertiseandgrace*

(I have deep concern for such dear friends)

we left for Hawaii in a first-class cabin
hung our suits on bronze hooks
buckled ourselves to the liner's luxuries

spilling coins into the Pacific all the way

5.

when I returned to the Occidental, alone,
only a month later
I secured the same suite,
and waitresses
returned to my bed appreciating Neil's absence
ran the tab through the roof thinking,
        Jesus! Praise Jesus! Why is this so simple?

when he arrived, eventually,
        pink as swine,
        burnt by Pacific air
        standing, winded, in the doorway,
        bracketed by two policemen
I pled innocence and shock
thanking god my maid was pointing
her nipples towards the door just then

the police turned politely away
and Neil sighed, long and steady,
staring,
understanding

they arrested me delicately,
mannered,
saying,
        Sorry sir. To interrupt you so –
        Just doing our jobs, like.
        For Mr. Neil, you know, sir. Sorry.

they deposited me in a cushioned cell
and fed me entrees from the hotel,
gave Neil dirty looks
when he inquired after my prosecution

I wrote to the *Post* claiming innocence,
enclosing the details of Neil's injustice

(the same envelope carrying stories
of my English riches, French soldiery, Indian charm

continents rubbing together all the way to the printing press)

6.
at the trial,
Neil decided to publicly believe in my England

I accepted the acquittal,
straightening my lapels,
marched straight back to the hotel
to apologize
and attempt compensation
in upper-class whisky, women,
the same view of the city's skyline

arriving,
officially,
· in San Francisco
my history stamped valid by the justice system

wholesale future
cradled in the arms of millionaires

7.
the first time I meet Eadweard I'm on assignment.
I share a table with him
at an artists' social

he invites me over for tea
once a week
for half a year

Flora serving, giving me blushes
spinning roses over crumpets

Flora, my heart
introduced as Eadweard's
only unpredictable problematic

it's at the Opera House
that I first relieve Mrs. Muybridge of her stale allowances,
I pluck her blossoms,
dry her rose petals in direct daylight

I plunge into her purse,
diving,
        her mouth, there, at the crest of waves
        instructing me

I hold her middle in the back rooms of chemistry shops
heat her ear with calculated exhales,
        spilling ethers across her back
        on the quick frictions of tabletops

she tastes the hot love of my scripts
acts the lover in letters
develops our romance in her dresses

in April, *when we were both so pale*,
I enter the stage,
then, finished,
deliver a punchline
refasten my trousers,
exiting the hotel in an uninterrupted streak
to the green room of the city
so

the seed in her stomach becomes a bullet
at the Yellow Jacket Mine

CUSPIDOR COPPINGER

1.
like Harry, Chinatown's streets are preoccupied

Ross Alley's pre-electric brickwork
hides me in a tin entranceway,
old hat outstretched, watching his shadow lengthen

> others pretend not to see him,
> allow his darkness by moving around it.

> this should have been me.
> I should have sunken into the mortar where I belonged,
> let his velvet outstrip my literacy.

but, as he passes, my cat spits out of the wall
and I follow, bend over the animal

> as I reach out to glove white fur
> retrieve the skeleton, gently as I can
> put him on my shoulder where he likes to be,
> I see what Harry's holding, subtly
> on the hip, like a revolver:

> a sign written in large, looping, cursive English

> and, before thinking, the language drips out
> without mathematics

> *What do you need?* I say
> hand on the cat, hat
> eyes on his penmanship

Larkyns pauses,
spins,
dramatic,
cat's claws digging through rags

the sign says this: *If you can read this, I want you.*
and he holds it a few inches closer to me, feet planted in shadow

I saw it the first time. What's in it for me?

his voice is skeptical, purposefully baritone:

What's your name?

I watch him, head still protected by shadows

Let me see your face. Are you a Chinaman?

when I stand, shifting focus from the sign,
the only sentence he gives me is

I dislike cats.

he illuminates the paper,
holds it between us:

1. *You must be able to read and write*
2. *You must enjoy the theatre.*
3. *You must be discreet.*
4. *A dollar a week and a private room, daily, with toilet.*

I unfurl my hand, freeing it from the hat,
reach

he looks at the cat

newspaper coming out of his cloak,
he asks me to read aloud from classified ads
    alley flooding with prices for cherry china cabinets,
    antique drafting equipment,
    odd lonely appeals of rich widowers

when I finish, he smiles,
removes a pencil from the plenitude of his pants
hands me paper, and asks me to describe the scene
    that I write out, complete with his entrance as the devil
    dark cloak personified,
    adverbs overused, adjectives flooding

       my writing voice doesn't match the rest of me
       and
       reading it, he smirks

    The cat, of course, would not be welcome indoors.

When I don't respond he follows my clavicle to the animal's body.
Exhales a slow sigh.

    Very well. I do know a good enough veterinarian.

Interrupts silence by offering his palm
our grips locking in the diffused gas light:

    my only victory.

I'm to attend three plays a week,
dressed in suits that will remain his property.

I'm to enter the theatre from the rear,
sit in the darkest sections,
exit immediately after the curtain falls.

I'll be given pencils and notepads,
and reviews should be written in formal language.
He doesn't tell me what these will be used for.
Keeps his motive inside him.

Hints at the workings of the clock
without revealing its machinery.

　　　My name is Coppinger.
I say
sound coating the alleyway's rice-paper light

　　　I'm American.

Harry grins again, conceals both signs inside his black jacket.
Folds the newspaper into a club, soaring back on his heels.

　　　Very good. Very good. Meet me here Monday night.
　　　Eight o'clock. Please.
　　　Tell no one.

This, with a well-defined stare, the white smile against starched collar.
And, eyes darting to walls, quietly.

　　　Thank you, Mr. Coppinger.

(I will discover, later,
that though he had strutted the entire district's skeleton
　　　crept past its bloodshot gates
　　　carrying two pistols and his shield of language
　I'm the only person who acknowledged him.

It's only later that I realize how firmly, knuckles white,
he held onto me, pretending ease
most Chinese having retired long before,
fearful of thieves and bylaw officers with clubs.

It's only later that I understand how
he looked me in the eye because he needed me.)

2.

for the next two months, I watch butcheries of Hamlet,
spell compliments across the *Post*'s pages,
impersonating Harry

he doesn't attend the plays

each performance produces from him
a list of those to be flattered

(front-lit scrims, polished veneers)

    he collects his pay,
    spoons me my dollar,
    criticizes

each evening, reviews loop from my pencils
their yellow bodies disappearing by the cat's napping,
each article printed under *Major Harry Larkyns*' name
in the paper's new drama columns

    I refuse to use erasers,
    giving the pages the truth of thought,
    unlocking the workings of words and leaving them exposed

    scratch of lead a kind of water music

3.
once,
I miss a performance

    (whisky)

Larkyns gets reprimanded, docked
storms towards my table,
cloak an angry cloud

he spreads his arms
scans the window, ceiling, the bare walls of the room
returns his vision to me, smiling
silently lifts the animal from its basket

when he breaks the cat's neck,
its blood shoots across my papers,
crunch of it muting the rasp of his breathing

he tosses its body into a corner where the window ends
shows me his angry teeth

corpse leaking its shadow into the floorboards
all afternoon

4.
I write the letter to the *Post*'s editor anonymously,
in the finest English I can imagine,
impersonating the reviewing voice I've used

I fingerprint the paper with details,
stamp evidence across the address
seal the envelope with the bronze stamp Larkyns insisted I use
when sending in columns
    hot, cardinal candle wax
    filling his personal calligraphy

I don't expose the entire truth of him
instead,
I measure the murder he's done,
balance it with language
cold stain in the room echoing the hot script in the envelope

    tertium non data

5.
when Harry is dismissed, he comes after me
the anger in his head, mechanical,
hands curled into talons

I position the cat on the table with its eyelids up
surrounded by pencils, draped in paper
shut the door behind me,
finally,
wearing his best jacket, its skin

    he will penetrate this room,
    approach the table by the window
    find, in consummate calligraphy,
    the bare message:

    My name is Coppinger, it says.
    I have your suit.

6.

San Francisco *Examiner*, October 19, 1874:

*From that time on, whenever Coppinger met Larkyns, Larkyns would
take him by the nose and the lower jaw, and spreading open his mouth
with a grip of iron, would spit down Coppinger's throat!*

*He was arrested for this and tried. When the jury heard the story of
Coppinger's baseness, they acquitted Larkyns amid the cheers of the
spectators.*

*It became the custom for no newspaper man to associate with Coppinger
and he continued to be the most despised man in San Francisco.*

7.

I wore the suit to a few more performances
continuing to write in Larkyns' voice
until they fired me

I took its skin into the street, then
stitched its embroidery
with grime

(the longer I slept in it, the truer it was)

when he gives me his saliva
I chase it with a black index finger,
take the poison out
and put its music across his jacket

these hurried circles of acidic stink:
another type of storytelling

FLORA (LARKYNS)

1.
(before the end of the poem)
as Eadweard slows, considering
I enter another chaos:
    Harry Larkyns
and
every movement he makes is unpredictable

I first see him (as you know)
at the Grand Opera House,
sleeping in one of the gilded balcony boxes
    the applause,
    waking him,
    is a cue
    and he stands,
    immaculate, calculated
having noted the celebrity of the *dramatis personae*

he leads the ovation, not bothering to look for followers

    the crimson of his cheeks, then,
        the same colour as the stage curtains
    careful folds of his tie matching the softness of his thighs
        beneath the dark trousers

his hands, collapsing on themselves,
perform everything Eadweard is unwilling to consider

2.
weeks later,
in the Montgomery Street hotel suite,
when I ask Harry for instructions,
for dinner
he laughs and guzzles a triple shot of liquor

slaps me on the backside and tilts his mouth open,
waiting for me there

the opposite of clocks

3.
Harry is the most beautiful man I've known,
soft hair,
soft speeches

    he weaves through public rooms
    by stitching them with stories
    gives speeches over putrid pot roasts,
    praising the perfection of chefs
    compliments the ugliest, best-protected children

but, it's not the actor in him I love,
the fraud,
    the well-suited histories,
    fictions of India-France-England
    Romance, gallantry

all of this I accept without endearment

what I love in him is
    his constant self-creation
    the movement from empty space
    to complete narratives

    not history,
    but historical ink flooding across paper

4.
in bedrooms, even,
clothes peeled from backs
how we continue
depends on his storymaking

the truth being less about what's real than what's right

      arrow of the story
      less important than its details

5.
once, when we're all still friends,
we're at Woodward's Gardens,
Harry, Eadweard and I,
and the gallery is loaded with landscapes

Eadweard says it's horrible, low-class, the death of Vision,
holds the pieces in his squints

Harry sidles up to summits, descends Mediterranean blues,
a steamer sailing across salon.

his lungs fill with trade winds
as he seats himself at scandalous luncheons,
imposes on family portraits
transforms each scene into vaudeville

      my choice, then:
      the particular pivot of Eadweard's lenses
      or Harry's tectonic arms

Harry spins me past Mexicos, into royal European
meadows he rushes Paris nightlines past me and I'm
laughing, can't stop and I'm
laughing and the room goes dizzy and
Eadweard's gone for his camera in a serious black blur and
returns as I finally slow in front of a painting of pigeons by
the California sea

    Eadweard sets up robotically,
    hangs a hat across the lens
    removes the shield from a negative holder,
    collodion coat

    in the gallery's viewing chair, he pretends to sleep,
    hat brim over his brow, shoulders slumped in feigned boredom
    (this will be the only time I remember him
        ever acting out a joke)

as I approach ground glass to complete the shot
Harry comes in behind me
rustles my skirt, breathes slowly into my neck so I laugh again
hot muzzle on my collar

we remove the hat, briefly,
from the lens, then replace it,
Harry against me while Eadweard acts at dozing

with the shot exposed,
we detach our middles, reluctantly,
create a distance between bodies

    Eadweard, emerging from his stale humour
    as though our smiling were for him

6.
when Harry and I navigate the midway, later
vendors mistake us for Mr. and Mrs.
and we stay silently affirmative

back at the gallery,
Eadweard watches our backs
slowly swallowed by the Saturday crowd

he soaks the self-portrait in some acidic concoction
kept bottled in the dark,
image clinging to glass as he rinses
waves fixing his sleep to permanence

I suppose he might have returned to the studio
to compare his sleeping performance
with the salon
so he stood where we did,
holding two versions of the scene

deciding which to trust

7.
I have the baby in the summer of 1874
in Oregon,
Eadweard sending me there
with a letter,
delivered from the middle of the state's wilderness
demanding

we name the newborn:
    Floredo Helios Muybridge

Harry there,
at my bedside,
with the birth certificate

(plot, plot, plot, plot, plot:
why do these chronologies insist so much?)

1.
Eadweard finds the first letter under Flora's pillow
leans so far into it that his back bends in half
    tries to steady the paper
    headache growing across irises

    Flora, in the kitchen, singing sunlight

2.
he stomps into her room, red-faced
attempting control
Flora sifting weightlessly across the floor
a bowl of apples in her hands,
soft manicure against the red rounds

when he smashes his shaking fist onto the table,
    Goddammed letter!
one of its legs breaks beneath him

Jesus Christ Jesus Christ woman
for sweet Christ's sakes!
the hand a stone
Flora frozen against cupboards

the bowl
broken into triangles across tile

apples fan across the floor
one bumping into Eadweard's shoe where his
pant legs shake

    his eye on her
    her eye
    on the fist

    Eadweard,
    what the hell are you doing?

3.
he ploughs through proper streets
startling horses, smashing into ribs
elbowing *Jesus Christ woman* corners
    stomach held out, beard over his shoulder
    still swearing, letter in his fist,
    a paper *goddammit goddammit woman* ball
running
up the final stairs to the newspaper's floor
with dark smudges beneath his arms
back gleaming beneath his suit jacket

    trying not to curse
    he needs to shape each phoneme
    consciously,
    the blood in his head:

    Ah, yes. Ex-cuse me. Ma-jor Ha-rry Lar-kyns, please.
    Is he in?

4.

Harry, immaculately dressed,
reclines in his chair
folding paper into cranes,
tongue sticking out the side of his mouth

Eadweard slams the paper onto his desk,
steps back noting the distance of walls, stairwells

Harry, not returning the stare
continues folding, says
> *You all right, chum? Sound a bit winded.*
> *Won't you sit down?*

Eadweard, breathing heavy contradictions into the office
Harry's chest puffed up, folding
> *What is it, old man? Theatre tickets?*

Eadweard is on him instantly
the papers on the desk falling in a cloud
> Harry against the wall beneath the older man,
> the creak of wood behind two backs

Eadweard fills one hand with his jacket
the other buried in Harry's hair
> even then,
> ripping,
> even then he is thinking
> that Harry is unusually soft,
> unusually plush
> the hair beneath his hand,
> like water

breathing into his face,
he pushes him straight to the floor
says,
quietly,

controlled
pronouncing each syllable

    I'll
    fuck
    ing
    kill
    you.
    Har
    ry.

smiling, now.
    You understand?

    You.
    Stay.
    Away.
    From.
    My.
    Wife.

Harry on the floor,
surrounded by paper

    half-folded bird
    still
    between his doughy
    fingertips

PLOT AND MELODRAMA

when Eadweard finds the second letter
he holds his fists tight as he can,
drops the hand with the paper to his side
rubbing his forehead with the other

he slips out one of the apartment's doors
padding on the sides of anonymous feet
hears
the lock click
against Floredo, starting to cry, waking, wanting milk
    Flora, in the kitchen, again

he launches into street
chin down, eyes up
running in unrelieved lines,
ninety-degree turns at corners

because Harry left town after the newspaper incident
disappearing into a tidy hillside office
to run a silver mine,
Eadweard can't find focus,
is adrift, seeking names and targets

when he finally arrives at Susan Smith's apartment
he is winded, toe rubbing awkwardly against leather
    the blister inside the sock
    bursting when he leaves

    (all this plot reported in the papers)

he knocks on the door three times
braces his feet against floor,
hears Flora's midwife approaching through a barrier of wood

Who's there?

Mrs. Smith, are you busy? I want to see you.

the door cracks open,
brackets Susan's wrinkled forehead, her hand holding a skirt
Eadweard brushing past her, bolt slipping into its strike plate

    he holds the letter up
    so sunbeams project its ink
    across the walls

    Tell me what you know, Susan ... I have rights.

she is frozen, fist clogged with cloth
they have never met before

    What have you got there, Mr. Muybridge? Another pause.
    I say, are you all right? Your hand is shaking so.

he spins, ferocious
backs her in an instant into the closed door
puts his hot breath into her face, skin stretched white

    I'm not a fool, Mrs. Smith.

    No. Of course not, I didn't mean...

    Mrs. Smith, if you don't tell me the truth
        I shall consider you a bad woman!

he puts his fist, with the letter in it
through the wall
inside the borders of things
    Susan still stiff against the door,
    watching him vanish into her rooms

when he finds the photo of Floredo
    he lifts the baby's face
    holding the mounted image
    towards the ceiling, wanting air
        room starting to shift

Who is it?

He is your baby.

I have never seen this picture before. Where'd you get it?
    Where was it taken?

    Your wife sent it to me from Oregon. It was taken at Rulofson's.

he breaks the frame while undoing it
glass dropping,
turns the paper over in his hands,
begins to shake, high Romantic, reading
in the tight, black flowers of Flora's script:

    Little Harry

aiming every muscle at the door, he comes at Susan with his fists up

she tells him everything, with quotations:

    Harry and Flora in bed, at hotels, at the theatre, studios
        sheets *in the laundry*

    Harry and Flora *concerned* that Floredo's hair would be
        too dark

    Flora and Harry planning to relocate to England,
        Mrs. Harry Larkyns

75

when the apartment doubles around him
he breathes a careful mist into the room's logic
drops to the hardwood (afterbirth of stereoscope)

     Susan thinks he is going to die

he rolls onto his back, across triangular shards
establishing boundaries

     bits of glass in his jacket

Susan nods, nervous
as he rises
unbolts the door to the hallway
     windows in his back catching radiance
     and throwing it back into the apartment

he descends
without wiping the salt from his face
losing the sense of smell, taste
chooses one of the streets he sees and tears into it
wanting desert

noon sun blinding pupils

Leaving San Francisco

Muybridge staggers uphill to the Bradley and Rulofson galleries,
where we meet him, at the start of things.
He's worked here for five years.
The door's brief yawn: Exposure.

He trudges across the room, causing several clients to drift out of
his path, their bodies a wake behind him. Rulofson, businessman
and owner, patron of the arts, curator, finds him waiting for the
elevator to the photography gallery. Muybridge has never taken it
before, doesn't trust it, worries its metal might close around him,
a belly.

Eadweard's pupils are wide.
He reaches out into the air, trying to rearrange particles.

Always conscious of his public, Rulofson invites him into a private
office, and Muybridge sees the customers for the first time, goes,
stares at floorboards.

Rulofson discusses the day's business. He reaches for a pencil on the
desk and tips over a vase of dead flowers, brown dripping across the
desk onto Eadweard's shoes. He mumbles apologies, rises, asks after
Mrs. Muybridge, bangs his head reaching for a napkin, drops it,
crosses the room to where Eadweard is still standing, shoe puddled
in flower roots, retrieves the napkin from its inertia.

Muybridge swings back the office door and is gone.

Rulofson finds him, again, by the elevator, eyes closed and red. When
he opens them, Rulofson, forehead wrinkled, carrying the dropped
napkin, is looking at him. Muybridge crosses the gallery to his own
office in a pure raking diagonal, customers sidestepping him.

Eadweard collapses in a chair, smelling lemon zest under his nails.
Says nothing.
He slides back a drawer and finds a pistol. Its steel against skin.
He brings it out onto the desk, tastes its oil, calculating weight.
Smith and Wesson. Number 2. Old army.
Rulofson gasping as he enters and sits.

One of us will be shot, says Eadweard.

Are you mad? What have you against me?

Eadweard tries again: *One of us*, he points vaguely out the door.

*Oh god. Eadweard, you have much to live for. You're a great artist.
Think of poor, lovely Flora. Think of Floredo!*

Rulofson has drifted backwards, accidentally, so his chair lurches
upwards, knees rising to his chin. His voice rises, too. Muybridge
sighs, points the pistol's barrel at him. Says, *No*. He pulls one of the
letters from a pocket, brings the paper to his face, smelling Flora
there, shoves it across the desk where Rulofson flinches, reaches
out, reads.

One of us will be shot.

Opening a drawer, Eadweard fingers six bullets. He places these in
a chest pocket like pencils. Folds greenbacks into his trousers, rises
silently, sticking the pistol under his belt at the small of his back.

Rulofson finishes the letter, holds it in his right hand.
With the napkin in his left, he looks ready to lead cheers.

You don't mean to kill him?

One of us will be shot.

Yes... But... Oh god, don't kill him!

Rulofson rustles his paper wings against air. When Muybridge moves to the door, Rulofson stands suddenly in front of him. Slipping slightly, he crashes into Eadweard's chest.

Eadweard! Many women are wrongly accused!

Muybridge shoves him aside, slams the door,
customers looking up from paintings.

When he reaches the salon's exit,
he goes through it in one swift moment, running.
A wound clock.

San Francisco passes him in a dream, streets clothing hills.

He follows Montgomery Street, what the newspapers later call *the guilty hotel*, galleries. Increasing his speed, the gears in his head turn over. He stops seeing city, reduces himself to direction and colour, has only the automatic exchange of balance in his legs. The slap of his feet against sidewalk, a metronome.

His rhythm digs the pistol's sight into his back in a blood crescent,
red moon rising on his jacket as he arrives at the sea.
The scar, later, is a collapsed bracket.

He boards the ferry at four o'clock,
still running even as he shifts from solidity to liquid,
translating the mechanics of concrete into the truth of water.

Boat's metal, whale's ribs.

ARRIVING AT VALLEJO

1.
it's thick midnight when the ferry docks
so Eadweard vacates the harbour relying on memory,
finds perimeters and trusts them

at the dock, he catches the last train,
rides metal into landscape
and steps into darkness

he hires a carriage to climb the ten miles and one thousand feet
up Mount St. Helena, to the Yellow Jacket Mine
where Larkyns is playing cards,
counting silver bars

2.
the driver uses his fingers for light
hold the reins, extending from his arm, an extra limb
	I know this country, he says, *don't worry*
cart's wheels released into the night's liquid gravity

	the stars are silver hints

Eadweard rolls the barrel of his pistol with a thumb,
clicks its machinery inside his jacket,
caressing metal, shutting its lens
handle fitting into palm

he fills its emptiness with the calm perfection of bullets

asking about highway robbery, he expels one shot
orange explosion igniting rolling hills
arm, steady, extended
as his locked elbow swallows the bullet's retort

at the peak of the mountain,
house perched like a nest,
the carriage takes its payment,
and slips behind geography

the windows of the mining cabin
paint yellow polygons onto the clearing
a party's music ending where Eadweard stands,
framed
in the entranceway

3.
man raising a pistol and firing

as the cabin's striped fire
shatters triangles
over the hillside,
Eadweard approaches the door
and a man undoes the wooden hinge

Muybridge shrinks from its yellow,
hand circling his gilded pocket watch
his language,
from the darker air
asking for *Mr. Larkyns*, please
saying his business will
  only take a minute, just a minute, thanks.

Harry excuses himself
from a game of hearts,
weaves through bodies
whisky breath
bringing his cards along to the door,
cigar clenched between molars

he tilts his face out into the soupy stars
laughs,
exhaling brown smoke around Eadweard's shoulders

> *Who is it, friend?*
> *It's so dark. I can't see you*

Harry lifts a thumb to his forehead,
cupping vision,
queen of spades against his cheekbone

> *Good evening, Major.*
>
> *My name is Muybridge.*
>
> *Here is the answer to the message you sent my wife.*

4.
Robert Bartlett Haas. *Muybridge: Man In Motion.*
    Berkeley: University of California Press, 1976:

Muybridge fired out of the darkness at Larkyns,
who fell at the base of a huge oak tree
at the entrance to the house,
struck below the heart.

Witnesses later claimed that Larkyns,
reeling back into the house,
had run through the kitchen and sitting room,
and then out the door, to fall by the tree.

But Dr. Reid,
who was summoned that night,
declared that Larkyns must have died instantly from the wound.

After firing,
Muybridge entered the house.

He surrendered himself immediately.
Then, turning to the ladies in the room, he said,
"I am sorry this little trouble occurred in your presence."

Some of the witnesses, however,
stated that
these were the last words of Harry Larkyns.

5.
at the funeral,
the audience litters the air with predictable tears.

they reach into the sky
and position Harry there

sing "Flee as a Bird to the Mountains"
holding him up

Flora's milk drying
on his grounded, glazed lapels

SUITS

Coppinger gets the news at the bar
before a half-filled pint
reacts
in the San Francisco *Examiner*, October 20, 1874:

A glass of beer stood before him.

Pushing it from him he called for a glass of something stronger, at the same time saying, "There is, indeed, a special Providence in the killing of that man. I drink to the special Providence."

This speech was so brutal, that the men who stood about placed their glasses on the bar and moved away. But the infamy was to go further.

This individual who had trembled before the deceased while he lived, went out and walked hastily to the rooms where Larkyns lay in his coffin. He gazed long and maliciously at the features of the dead, and then turned and walked out, rubbing his hands and grinning like a human jackal.

Outside the door he spoke in a voice loud enough for all about to hear him, "I'd walk twenty miles the stormiest night that ever was to gaze on that sight!"

this, in large type
beside the obituary where
Larkyns is called a

    gentleman in the truest sense of the word,
since
    vulgarity of every kind was a perfect stranger to his soul

distinguished, heroic, unselfish, generous
moving through life *nobly, grandly*

    a musician of culture

Harry's holy adjectives against Coppinger's straight plot:

    two suits,
            full house

ALBUM IV:

BRANCH
LINES

In the Napa County Jail Cell

the window bars are loose
so Eadweard's capture is a matter of choice

his hair goes completely white

cradling his quill's calcium
he dips its tip into an inkwell
circles the feather around his mouth, tasting dust

he scratches letters over the grains of handmade papers
each small pellet of bark,
mountainous across the desert of the page
the hollow where his quill holds fast to its feather
used to be wings,
used to be a bloodline to the sparse heart of a gull

> the letters he writes from this grey square
> are heavy with this misdemeanour
> dove's blood looped into every capital

he takes his dinners in silence
removes silver covers from entrees with calculated effort,
placing them,
cautiously,
across dinner trays, over napkins
avoiding sound,
intentional
utensils joined only in the choreography of his teeth,
patient grind of food a machinery he can trust

the slow decay of his body is a broken pulley

when he emerges, for court
he carries his pen,
hides forks in his pockets
holds his watch in a hand's hollow,
relying on its weight

three months of prison measured by
the white whiskers that collapse from his jaws
like water

Contemplation Rock

1.
at the trial, Eadweard's famous lawyers work without legal fees
believing in a certain morality of ownership

they plead *temporary insanity,*
have the court record the proclamation,
invite doctors,
jury watching Eadweard's fixed skeleton
and not believing it

on the first day,
Rulofson bumbles into the room, dropping papers.
he holds a snapshot of Eadweard perched
    on the kerb of a mountain
says,
      No sane man, excusing me, your honour,
      would ever venture to such a precipice.

    Eadweard, silent on the bench, never forgives him for it

the driver who skirted Mt. St. Helena
describes the orange flash of a bullet against rolling terrain

men detail where the bullet's peak dismantled Harry's chest
Muybridge disappearing in smoke

when Flora speaks, the crowd goes quiet:
    I've known Eadweard to be so focused, so utterly tuned to one thing
    that he's stayed awake all night reading the classics!

doctors with drawings of frontal lobe trauma
hold legal bills for Eadweard's suit
against the Butterfield Stage Company
    make spirals against their temples, pointing at him
    saying the collision made him unable to distinguish things
    made him take unsafe risks, ossified his senses

someone tells the story
of Eadweard bursting into the newspaper office
Harry holding the paper crane

even Silas T. Selleck
moustache a wriggling caterpillar as he speaks
raises arms, calls his old friend
    eccentric and wavering

saying that Eadweard was never the same after the accident
that he
    returned to California strangely quiet
    would spend hours staring at the edges of an object,
    tight-lipped and rapt

jury looking from eyewitness to the fixed defendant:
    parallax

2.
Eadweard rejects the plea
so
in their closing statements,
his lawyers accuse the twelve jurymen
of hypocrisy
saying they should

> *Imagine their own wives with some fiend in fine linens*
> *perhaps, even now, stroking the china in their homes,*
> *holding their women against windows,*
> *whispering.*

he details how Eadweard is left alone, now,

> *forever*

with only his career to love

ends the speech shouting
NATURAL RIGHTS! and
Amen!

so that,
after two hours of
pacing,
punctuating,
pointing,
when the defence rests,
the room explodes in applause

windows shaking against all that yellow

VERDICT

the forks and watch in his pockets, Eadweard rises

as the paper dawdles from the judge's hand
back to the dry palm of the jury foreman,
he massages metal, relying on curves

>they've taken thirteen hours, overnight to decide
>voted three times, unable to structure the exact psychology
>of naming

total silence as they unfold the paper to read the verdict
in three even syllables:

>*Not guilty.*
>(the last admitted California killing
>ever acquitted without madness)

the room is voices
Eadweard's spine crumpling into a twisted ball,
a Victorian train wreck
to match the dramatic O his mouth makes

>when he tries to thank the jury,
>his back sags improperly,
>lungs deflating against applause

every gentleman in the room turns away from his white, wet beard

they carry his body out on a stretcher
where the doctor,
trying to steady a hand against the heaving chest,
says, angrily
    I sympathize with you
    but this exhibition of emotion is extremely painful to me,
    and for my sake alone I wish you to desist.

Muybridge looks up at him,
white locks against the brown leather sofa,
silently straightens his spine to an acceptable rigidity

retreats from the overcast room to an authorized door

where the crowd's ethical cheering lifts him down those steps
to the sea

COPPINGER THINKING AT THE JACKSON STREET JOSS HOUSE

1.
still in Harry's suit,
I puncture the temple's skin
tiptoe towards altars
where fat buddhas smile
around wildflowers
(without English)

the smell of Harry's pockets,
overpowers the bodhisattvas' metals
I kneel and take a statue's toe in the gears of my teeth
(brown dent left on its foot)

I light sticks on the shrine's candle
        sandalwood meeting soiled jacket
        prayers
        (a product of boundaries)

when I rise
a man drifts past me in grey robes
a monk's cane, kite's truss
across his back
his fabric a casual, silver sail
everything about him is air

        (that's why I lift him up in memory
        to the spare density
        of birds)

he stumbled
staring at my pinstripes,
the brown evidence of city across my collar,

gravel in the crafted entranceway
beneath his slippers
(a reminder of Earth)

2.
I'm thinking that
the history we make here is thick
(so that every exhale makes legends
 legible)

I'm thinking that
a lyric is planted in
each
careful
stone
(so that walking is a hymn
 to motion)

I'm thinking that
even urinating, here,
makes a yellow singing in the bowl
(gravity holding it in its hands,
 California gold)

3.
        as I filter into the street's sewage, opium haze,

            (I'm remembering that my cotton skin belongs to a corpse)

        I'm thinking that the bullet sleeping in Harry's chest,

            (shaped precisely like these stones)

        is an echo of our conjugations:

            (an occidental period at the end of)

                    a true sentence

Boarding an Exit: February 27, 1875

1.
just days after the trial
Eadweard's boat is a spoon
in the bay's foam

he parts surfaces
body framing the sky's round

the clipper that's swallowed his hardware
is a steel cliff
his longboat inching towards it,
aware of the explosions that exist
in silence
     his equipment,
     boxed and secretly seeded in the hold,
     waiting to detonate

2.
with a swell, he grips portside rope
just as the sails
switch to more commanding gears of wind

the taxi slices itself away from the towering hull
Eadweard hanging by the side of the vessel,
     uprooted

3.
when he finally climbs up,
legs splayed over a metal railing,
stewards appear to take his hands in theirs
    the emergence, then,
    a kind of ballet,
    smell of salt in his jacket

he elevates perspective
    ascends to the upper deck
    holding his ticket in front of him,
    a shield

4.
below deck,
his stowaway cameras are set to record
what's left:

        breakers against boat's arrow;
        Yosemite riverbed narrows

        sky's patched whiteness;
        gunpowder chart

        cell's barred window;
        Yellow Jacket heart

        bulge of land against the bay's waves;
        Flora's hip against rib cage

this way
stereoscopes rhyme Eadweard's exit,

slow seeds
swallowed
by a murder
of crows

Part Two: ,

Volcan Queszaltenangeo, Guatemala, 1875.

[Central]

ALBUM I:

MAPS

Reading the Plaza of Antigua

1.

All across the frame, people have refused capture. Their bodies, brief streaks of light across the market's noise. Bodies arriving at the paper's surface from the hills as though they'd dropped from the background, clothing burdening the scene with contrast.

Eadweard uses their blurs. Some have stood, perhaps, for hours, under a certain shadow, and (seeing Eadweard load the camera) have jumped from permanence. Their bodies are ghosts, buildings' bones seeping through flesh, half-exposed.

This contour line is a woman, haggling. This whirlwind of white light, a boy spinning in place. This silver banner, a man who's just exited the frame to walk ten miles back to his village, up the side of the volcano, towards sky. Two specific legs support a burst of fluorescence, where a figure has bent to the mud in an automatic semicircle, disturbing the foreground with waves. The dance of a young woman in a white dress paints a halo behind a fixed, staring farmer. *Angelus novus.*

Eadweard's thumb must've traced the gradual background slope of *Volcan Agua* against the air before framing it in the top half of the focal plane. He must have positioned the *Palace of the Captains General* intentionally, so its highest corner just grazes the background's pitch, a meeting of territories. Volcanic throat against stone's collarbone.

2.

Like Eadweard, I'm trying to fix blurs, to translate continuity. Like Eadweard, I want permanence, names. I lean into the paper's grain, smell dust lifting from the book, beams falling through the window into the centennial bodies breathing there. This image, traveling the entire North American mainland, over a hundred years of distance, to find me here in the particular latitude of a Canadian afternoon.

Whiteness around the print, marking possibilities.

In the picture, baskets perforate cloth geometry, balanced on heads, giant nails digging into dirt. Every stall is covered by the slant of a square umbrella, each reflecting the sun in a white shine. The squares float like paper drifting in the development bath, sides curled from the acids' work. Your eye can hop from one to another without dipping into the river of bodies. Or, you can circulate, continue from umbrella to umbrella, around the plaza. Slip, if you like, from the surface into liquid and lose your boundaries.

(The most important time is happening between categories.)

Translating a Map of Guatemala, 1875

1.

When Eadweard first steps from the boat's Pacific swell to southern Guatemala, he enters a mirror. Cliffs reflected in the water's shoreline. He sees emerald bridges emerging from the ocean and forgets justice, quick rise of peaks cutting off his history.

The country's southern coastline spreads itself from Mexico to Panama, folding most of its towns—*Antigua, Atitlán, Quetzaltenango, Totonicapán*—across the Western Highlands, where Eadweard tours, circumambulating lakes with thatched permanence, reaching into volcanoes for deliverance from the white heat of Catholicism.

Thirty years before Eadweard arrives, Rafael Carrera, a twenty-five-year-old *ladino*, delivered an administered peace to the *indios* here; invented school systems, fertilized farms, held villages in his vision and forced them onto maps. He took pieces of his body from Europe and translated them, removed his Spanish boots and left them below arches of colony. He celebrated native enclosures of *cochineal*, picked the fiery blood of cactus fields and ate it, planted supposedly kind authority on every mountainside. When he died in 1865, fifty-one years old, the whole country went thirsty, wanting to spread his red brine across its skin. They drank the new government's poison, slow drunken tilt of afternoons spent remembering something apparently perfect, before. Eadweard thinks everything they say now comes in the sad voice of drink, thick tongues curving unsuccessfully around syllables, confused by the spaces necessary in language, mouths so full that words come out dull and broken. Carrera.

Coffee has preceded Eadweard by decades, and its evidence surrounds him, steeping. Wherever he goes in Guatemala, yawning branches rake against him, white blossoms colonizing his nostrils like talcum powder, berries hanging in smooth ovals against the scent of growth. Fruit hardening in the sun like bullets.

In 1875, as Eadweard disembarks, Spanish churches are crumbling into shadows, old bureaucracies stained white. Bones. President Barrios establishes the first national bank in a neoclassical quadrangle, capitalizing Progress, imports enormous, steam-powered coffee grinders, forces children to new plantations, sells ancestries to Germans, English, Texans. The Pacific Mail Steamship Company delivers capital, Panama Rail delivers a trickle of careful tourism, the soil delivers grounds. Coffee beans are carried to ships by ox cart and Mayans, exchanged for corn that's now imported from Mexico to feed plantation workers during well-choreographed breaks. New, iron rakes (for turning sun-dried beans) form calluses on men's palms that blister in the work's friction, skin deformed into white pockets. The whole country collapses into one industry, one export, beans delivered across the world in hand woven sacks to the golden cups of royalty. Brown dressed in sugar. Mornings, through verdant leaves. Afternoons in blossoms. Evenings picked. Dark blood berries. Midnight black machines. Lantern glow.

Eadweard stays here for nine months, following the scent of berries, framing more than four hundred images. He climbs the lips of volcanoes, rounds empty alpine paths and finds entire villages naked, washing a week's cloth in a river's current. He tours towns to record ruins, burns blurred citizens onto glass, holds markets in his lenses, arches echoing land. He drifts through the avenues of Spanish cemeteries, holds a child's outline in his hands to shape it beautiful with light.

He melts into landscape and recreates himself: *Senor D. Eduardo Santiago Muybridge*, jungle journalist, coffee cartographer.

Everything he makes is self-portraiture.

2.

(Eventually, all of the buildings he photographs in 1875 are destroyed by earthquakes, the major shakings later recorded in bold timelines, as though their years were self-explanatory events: *1877, 1902.*

The lustre Muybridge captures is the only evidence we have of this architecture, volcanic sheen, ramadas. The surf he blurs has evaporated. Each clear face is a stopped ghost, permanently doomed in the present tense. *Dead,* and *going to die.*)

coactlmoctl-lan: Land of the Snake-Eating Bird.

Guatemala: The Land of Trees.

VOLCAN QUETZALTENANGEO

1.

When I undo the book's fold, I confuse the volcano there with a
scientific photo of the attitudes of clouds. The steam rising from a
ring of molten rocks is a midday sun emerging through thunderheads
above a bay's rugged shoreline. The rocks are continental black, the
largest coal vein in the world.

Eadweard had positioned himself so that all the shapes in the
picture are abstract. He wanted this confusion, oxygen and pumice
mixed. Sealed the plate with boulders to erase landmarks. Steam
curling against solidity. Ash encircling air.

2.

When he finds the lava flow, Eadweard makes another picture of
the limits of things. Inserts ocean into the stubbornness of rock,
prints the empty centre, thinking of boundaries. Sweat dropping
from his beard to the caldera's lip.

At the crater, he picks up a bead of obsidian and holds its heat in his
fist, gripping energy. When he drops it back into its orange pool,
his white flesh opens.

3.

The scar later reminds him that movement exists
        in even the most permanent of bodies.

It sleeps in handshakes, surrounds his signature,
        runs itself over his gearing.

Every letter formed around
        this drumlin of knowledge in his lifeline.

A Roadside Scene, San Isidro

Having retreated from sea to jungle, Eadweard rises from a nap, lifting his flat body vertical. Claws colour away from his face, surfacing from leaves, the camera already set, waiting to photograph rivers. The colour that surrounds him is the deepest he's ever seen, midday clothed in a midnight sarong. He approaches the river through velvet trees.

In the smooth stream: Female quintuplets in identical dress. Scarlet cloth folded against five brown stomachs.

Eadweard sweeps towards his bottles, uncorks them, coats a plate, its edge catching a silvered ray and sending it across the bank to the women. He waves, returning stares, brushing twigs from his legs. The thicket where he slept has stained his trousers. The women carry wooden bowls, and one steps into the current, spoons a cup of motion out and pours it over her shoulders.

Ready, Eadweard wades in, smiling, his sweat green. He approaches cautiously, hands held out and unprotected. Bowing slightly, he raises palms again, removes his hat and places it on a stone. The women stare, hair trickling over their shoulder blades. Eadweard points at the camera, digs a fist into a pocket and brings out five copper coins, setting them in a line on the riverbank. The women watch. Eadweard points to the coins, and one of them rises to collect them. They disappear into the red cloth in seconds, faces never leaving his gadgetry.

Eadweard positions the women in a steady crescent from centre to left foreground.

The first woman, with waves just wetting her toes, is the furthest away. The second, three feet into the current, water capturing the mystery of her feet there, arms slightly up, holding a bowl. The next he turns around, another three feet closer, placing her hands on an inverted bowl over her head, hair an arrow towards the buttock's bluff. The fourth woman, another three feet foregrounded, holds the bowl in the identical pose, faces the viewer, mouth a split fruit. He places the final body, very excited now, beside the scene, in profile, foreshortened, stream capturing the time between bodies.

When Eadweard hurries from the river to the focal plane, back up the bank, his shoes bleed a dark gash across the dirt. The sequence simulated. The scene thought.

In the picture, time extends from the far bank to the river's middle to the viewer. The gradient of identical women becomes the record of one woman's movement. A history of her journey towards the bowl's coolness. Recorded. If you transplant the trajectory of women, you get the exact route of Eadweard's tour through Guatemala's map. Each body is a major town in the Sierra Madre. Bodies over distance. Details against the river's blurred mirror.

When Eadweard exposes them, he is thinking that value happens mostly in differences. That even the smallest action changes the whole slope of a map's future.

Ancient Sacrificial Stone, Naranjo

1.

In the cornfield, Eadweard trudges over broken stalks drying in afternoon heat. He confuses their cracks, looks at his feet, expecting to find his bones, snapped. Etches his name into a brittle trunk, imagining skeletons.

2.

He had risen over a hill to see the stone, its two o'clock shadow. Shaped like a giant tooth, it stands eight feet across and nine high, ending in a sharpened peak, occupies most of the photo. Dark triangle centred in the rectangular print, a flag.

Cut through its centre is a worn hole, size and shape of a human head. Eadweard imagines jugular blood washing over the rock, licking dirt where the granite base collides with horizon.

3.

Positioning one of his porters behind the portal, Eadweard asks him to remain very still, speaks English, expecting the Guatemalans carrying his equipment to understand him. They do, and a man arranges his skin behind the hole, face's range contrasting the flat plaster of the rock's roughness. Eadweard shoots him thinking blood is the colour of coffee berries. Man in the portal very serious: from his perspective, he's watching prehistory.

(Eadweard was wrong about sacrifice. This is a time machine.)

4.

Naranjo is an astronomy field.

People came here as farmers and left as students of the sky. They measured its offerings, carved the mathematics of seasons into animal hides. They sculpted serious holes in shale shields and held them to their faces, trying to focus on one aspect of one night. Charted orbits across millennia. The stone, an observatory.

Here, scientists confused rock with the hips of lovers, indifferent romantic air above their blue unions, ruddy paint on cheekbones. They watched stars drift across this portal, marked each with a spiral, remembering other seasons, predicting futures. Fearing rain, perhaps, they drew dry constellations across corn husks with chalk, carried them like broken children to the urgent safety of rooftops. The giant tooth in the cornfield, a door.

(Eadweard's expertise in clouds and moon exposures doesn't let him realize this. He concentrates so hard on details that he loses his horizons. Confuses stars with murder. The entropy of frames.)

5.
If he'd waited for twilight, had swung around the rock, held its coolness with his forehead, easing into the orifice, waiting for Venus to emerge on the blue bulb of the air, he'd have been able to mark the precision of specific stars. Recorded a thousand years of travel to that moment, that night, this angle.

The distance of the present. The presentation of distance.

Perhaps, in the right light, wind, the stars would be nitrate molecules in the night's glossy calm. Eadweard, at the portal, steadying his view on the bead of a revolver. Cornfield transforming itself from Guatemalan to Californian landmarks. Forest bleeding yellow triangles, mines.

He would see, perhaps, a bullet, marking the distance between his shield and target, its arrow permanent in the air between this safety and that inertia. His *my god my god* intentions encapsulated in the tiny missile that hung in air, exact. The boulder's window, the pistol's sight. Smell of Flora in the moonlight.

Round shroud of talcum circling the granite tooth.

ALBUM II:

LAS NUBES

1. 20(4) photographs

i.

Of the twenty-four official views he takes of *The Clouds*, a coffee plantation in the Guatemalan highlands, Eadweard only eventually publishes twenty, tracing the coffee-making process from seed to export. The four extras are not approved. The plantation owner calls them bad publicity, says they're awkwardly rendered, unfair, anti-modern.

These negatives Eadweard never prints, keeps in a silver safe in San Francisco. Four years later, after the fire, they're the only proof he was ever here, sealed into city below an old studio, earth swallowing them in 1906, knowing the value of seeds.

These four lost negatives are taken secretly, subjects unaware of the technologies shooting them from behind oaks, scree, the safe porches of rich *ladino* men armed with American pistols (I have no proof of this). If I'd have been there, I'd be able to give you their details, take you into their complete hearts.

Instead, in absence, we need to rely on likelihood, put faith into the science of logic. Eadweard translating realities into representations, sweating.

He would have included these images because he couldn't discriminate. He digested scenery whole. Captured what's real in order to forget its politics.

ii.
Eadweard slips into thoughtfully planted lines, unifies parallels, fictionalizing symmetry. The workers, pleasantly picking weeds, planting seeds, clearing, transplanting, weeding again, harvesting, sacking, soaking, drying, raking, re-sacking, bagging, naming, grading.

Pleasantly.

European owners watch over every gesture, their faces eased by shadows, carefully included in every picture. Their stiff figures placed in the backgrounds of each shot, meant to resemble armed fathers. *Mandamiento.*

iii.
In Antigua, workers tell Eadweard an old owner was dumb enough to inspect his land without guards. The evening men, emerging from tidy rows, hacked him to pieces, scattered his body parts across the depleted grounds to fertilize drooping bushes. Knives falling against his outline.

The Mayan women, they say, often take European lovers, cling to them, doting, rubbing sweat from toes. Their husbands watch foremen enter their homes and remove bodies.

Those women who don't choose "protectors" are marked, visited—*everyone knows this*—then docked a day's pay for lack of production, afterwards.

One woman protested in public Spanish. Enraged, the plantation owner was forced to hunt for the *ladino* rapist to scold him (with whisky) and reprimand him (politely). The time it took to find him (six hours, twenty-five minutes), sauntering across the orchards picking particular thighs out of the dark green branches, was added to the debt already owed. An entire week's pay withheld for language.

Children who return from harvest with half-filled baskets are beaten in front of their mothers.

Men who attempt escape are shot, bodies dragged into the shacks of workers, left there at the centre of things. The orphaned families are whipped, sanguinary sentences seeping exclamations across their backs. *This problem is not solved,* they say, *remember that.*

(In his albums, Eadweard would have stressed this, aesthetically. Would have taken an exact exposure to accentuate black blood dripping from the whip's wet tongue, dark gashes echoed by background cascades. The sight of a pistol against the temple of the worker, on his knees in the public lunch hall, contrast of metal against skin, dark shadows of his tongue echoing volcanoes. The child whose leg was being sliced in two because he was late delivering a message to his foreman, wet sawteeth gripping light as a mountain peak might. European fingers digging into a Mayan nipple so a rich halo emerges on the chest, a blossom. Other workers continuing the harvest all over the foreground.)

iv.
Behind these depictions, women, hidden amongst heavy foliage, veil the air with music, occasional pistol shots as percussion, constant patter of fresh berries dropping into baskets, a kind of rain. Work hymns.

But Eadweard's emulsions are silent. The voices, submerged.

This is why, scratching his name into corners, Eadweard must have been humming, must have been marking the scenery's signature. *Carrera* there in the bodies, singing out rhythmic histories. Women slowly covering their breasts in riots of white cloth, full scores.

Nothing Eadweard has will let him understand this music.

He makes the pictures to listen.

2. *Another bean history*

Eadweard stays in the plantation house owned and operated by a man named Mr. Willie Nelson (I'm not inventing this). Every sentence Mr. Nelson forms ends in some sort of exclamation, arms expansive. Everything he says is too loud. The house covered in sentences.

The morning Eadweard arrives, Nelson points to an etching hung above the fireplace. *Kaldi!* he says. *Goddamned goatherd who discovered coffee! In the dark continent! Long before Jesus!* The shepherd dancing with goats who stand on hind hooves and smile, drugged and hyperactive. Kaldi holds a thin pipe, grins. *That's where this began, you know!* he says. *We're returning these here dark folks here back to their roots!* His laugh is a wheeze. He continues. Says, in legends, Kaldi's typical goats didn't return one evening. He found them, evolved, having chewed the leaves of an Ethiopian shrub covered in berries. The next day, goats still waltzing, he declared the fruit safe, chewed, adrenaline pumping as he waltzed, envious of hooves.

From there! Nelson says, *The A-rabs got hold of the trees! Had 'em in their courts, a royal drink! Took some time for the rest of Europe to smuggle them seeds out!* He slurps at his mug. *One French feller, lost in the Atlantic doldrums for weeks, gave all his drinking water to a single pirated shrub!* Extends a well-clad arm towards the windowsill. *That's! I think! The source for most of the coffee we got here! That one French feller! Now! Of course! Coffee's as far from A-rabs as…Well! You're American, right?!*

Eadweard stays very still. Says, *I'm English,*   *actually.*

Frowning, Nelson points to a Mayan woman that Eadweard hadn't noticed, hidden on a mirador. Says, *The Indians are best handled as if they were children!* With this cue, the woman materializes holding a flat iron pan. For the next twenty minutes, she stirs the captured beans on the fire as they slowly brown, pop. She dumps their darkness into a mortar and smashes the drum into a fine powder. Laces a pot with grounds, boiling water, pouring into a tiny cup fringed with sugar. Rattles the last drops so foam appears on the surface, instant espresso. Disappears into the wall.

Mr. Nelson is smiling, still talking, he's been talking the whole time Eadweard watched the woman work, trying to translate her. With the cup in his hand, raised, Eadweard comes back to the conversation, where, with gusto, Mr. Nelson is saying, *A-rabs!* again, still frothing about the *Boston tea party!*, still laughing at Eadweard's being *A Real! Live! Brit!*

The drink burns Eadweard's tongue, and he smiles at its liquefied sugar, thinking of India-France-England. Thinking that every extravagant man he meets gives him a full spread of arms, a warning of wings.

3. Clearing ground for a coffee plantation.

This is how the land is taken.

A gang of children, armed with metal, invades the hillside. They've been taught to open a forest at the most efficient, most difficult thicknesses of trunk, to spread across the jungle, planting waves. Each tree is chopped until it begins to shift, lose confidence; child moving on to the next shaft, dismantling.

Later, the foreman, searching. He urges his strength over roots, examining, attempting to determine inertia. He is allowed time, unlike other workers, because his decision is essential. He considers every crown and trunk, calculates probability.

When he finds the giant master plant, he scans the horizon, memorizes a path for exit, aims at the splintered wound children have left in the wood. Raising his axe, he releases a series of arcs, slicing at weak space, a mathematician of forestry. When finished, he tosses the axe through his predetermined escape route, places both palms on the bark, throws the whole tree over, and runs.

If calculated correctly, this gravity key will cause every other standing structure on the hillside to collapse, will force the whole crowd into graves. As the foreman emerges into his clearing, an anthem of pines will explode against his ears. Dust clothing him, fogging the sun in a sickly yellow scum. The hill shaking for five minutes, twisted driftwood corpses strewn across the land: dead, stupid soldiers.

As the forest falls, the afternoon will fill with quetzals—the national bird. Sound of them lost in deciduous explosions. Streaks of colour across the yellow air.

After three weeks of drying, the bodies will be set ablaze. A burning battlefield.

These armies, wanting rain.

4. *peaberry*

When he finally escapes Mr. Nelson that first morning, Eadweard approaches *The Clouds* as though surfacing from depth. His hand, held aloft, guarding against obstacles, protecting. Arm an arrow to the oval he plucks from the lowest branch.

Eadweard rolls the supple crimson over his tongue. When his molars part the pulp, red bursts from the cherry, mucilage dripping into his throat, a bitter delta. He works his bones through the outer layer, finding a hard middle. Spits. The planted flesh shrinking into a subterranean husk, a buried wing.

In his mouth, he finds only one bean instead of two, cherry half empty. A *peaberry*. This botanical solace happens only when coffee crops are grown in exhausted soil, exposed to poisons, disease, can't weave their branches towards effective photosynthesis.

Still, the single living seed, beneath its flesh, is surrounded by a typical exoskeleton. Eadweard collapses on this shell, and the parchment splits. He chews, drops its casing to his guts, scratching his throat.

On his tongue, the tiny bean is surrounded by its final envelope of tough protection, the *silverskin*, a tight phyllo pastry around the hidden green. A calcium covering. He bites this last resistance, wanting bitterness. The naked bean's middle, where nourishment used to flow from the caffeinated stem, a canal through the half-dome's deserted flatness.

(Every surface Eadweard breaks ends up covered in silver.)

5. First day of the coffee season.

At the beginning of the working day, five a.m. and cold, Eadweard places two structures in the upper corners, uses them to balance, parenthesizing bodies.

The centre occupied by ladders, set up.
Their triangles ending in fixed baskets, waiting for fruit.

Behind each ladder is a still woman, looking through steps. Each body is sectioned, precisely cut. A landscape of torsos. Each pair of calves paralleled.

All the arms up.
(The bones beneath history)

6. brown mathematics

i.
Assuming escape from frost, flood, mutilation, drought, disease, a coffee tree is six feet high after three years of nurturing, an average North American male. Moved to shaded fields, it begins to bear fruit. After six more years, it is mature, doubled, and if fed appropriate minerals, transplanted by women to a permanent site below higher branches and pruned to allow the right amounts of daylight in, it continues to produce berries for fifteen to twenty years. Like Eadweard, once a tree reaches maturity, it stays there as long as it can, focuses on one sequence across calendars before dying.

Mark Pendergrast: *"On average—depending on the tree variety and growing conditions—one tree will yield five pounds of fruit, translating eventually to one pound of dried beans"* per harvest. (So, in a completed lifetime, the ideal specimen produces only twenty petite paper bags of husked, cleaned, dried and roasted beans.)

(Pickers know these numbers): *"Tiny women, perhaps four foot five inches, can carry amazingly large bags, twice their 80 pound weight. Some of the women carry babies in slings around front; after they dump their loads, they rearrange the babies on their backs… A good adult picker can harvest over 200 pounds of cherries a day."* (200 pounds, 40 stripped trunks, 3 ½ years of a single American kitchen. In a week, 1 woman picks an entire lifetime of my addiction.)

ii.

By 1876, in the space between Eadweard making these pictures and printing them, North America will have imported 340 million pounds of beans, harnessing one-third of the exports from every coffee-producing country in the world. By then, Guatemala will be sending over one-half of its exports to the USA, channelling hope into a single shipping lane. President Barrios learning English in whitewashed Guatemala City, concentrating his policy on sales, forgetting that to grow these beans at all, he relies on volcanic ash, the caffeinated shrubs only taking root in a certain mixture of lava and soil. Wanting progress, he forgets the violence in geology, the possibility that his topography could disintegrate: faults below his agriculture, slipping over themselves. Cracked glass.

The New York Coffee Exchange produces other earthquakes. Bumper crops create low prices. Disease produces rarity. Clients cheer when Central American forests collapse with failure. The more weight the workers are paid for, the less likely they are to get good money next year.

I sip my cup thinking of volcanoes.

7. *Canadian Silverskin*

i.
The sealed beans sleep in my plastic refrigerator.

I fish into the bag, hook harvests in a metal scoop, deposit them into a grinder.

Blue lightning leaps from the wall into the circular blade, destroying a lineage of berries.

I carry the dirt to the recyclable strainer without thinking of Antigua, release the tap's valve so that Canadian lakes can enter the sink, level the pot with filtered freshness. The pressure of water through grounds.

I carry the cup with me to Eadweard, crack open his spine and anaesthetize images. When I spill a puddle across one of his sky-shades I make a new thunderhead there.

ii.
For five years, I fill recycled notebooks with caffeine, steep myself in libraries, wanting details. Each word I make here is fuelled by ancestries of berries.

But, as I drink, I lose the red of cherries, just as a diver, entering the sea, will lose the red in sunlight. Everything at depth eventually appearing brown, turquoise. Pressure reducing the spectrum to shades.

Each submerged line I make ends up sepia-toned.

Each of Eadweard's translations shaped around my mug's easy water.

Teeth gone yellow in this refracted light.

8. *Bringing in the day's coffee picking.*

After several weeks wandering the uniform fields, Eadweard returns to his quintuplets.

He hears them there, in the ordered rows, singing, invisibly. The heavy notes rise past *The Clouds*, condensing in his ear canal. He waits, pulled into a tight ball, until the day ends, trails the women back to a weighing station, wanting his joy flattened.

Even with those collodion bottles in his palms, he can smell the berry juice on their fingers.

Ten women spread across the dirt, blocking.

As before, he approaches the scene pointing to his camera. He removes his hat, runs a wrist over his sternum. With gestures, he positions baskets on heads, pivots bodies into profile. He alternates the quintuplets with other women, thinking imagery, wanting each stage captured.

Arranges lives like fruit on a table.

He centres a figure dumping her brilliant ruby cherries into a grainy box.

Something in her face is stone. Her stiffness, a decision. Her back to the hut where an overseer stands, shadowed, hand, again, on hip. Her expression carries the knowledge of that pistol, whip. Memories of entrance. She translates nothing. Blank understanding in the mouth. Gives us her face, knowing.

(We're watching her.)

9. *Mill at Las Nubes. Las Nubes Coffee Mill.*

Two versions.

In the first, the jungle. Jade canopy against crimson sunset, mill centred, distant outline built on the tops of banyan trees. Plot. The top half is full of dark shapes that might be mountains. You confuse, this way, air with land. Motion of the tiny wheel at the bottom right of the building completely lost in undergrowth.

In the second, we're beside the building, close up, and its logical structure takes over. Jungle is used only to suggest periphery, vegetation ringing the primal object of construction. The wheel tumbles creeks over its hollows. A comma.

Eadweard places these dry photographs against each other, seeking rivers.

He constructs the building without humanity, places animals against planks, respecting pack mules and oxen as equivalent to horses. He writes this fact in letters, praising beasts of burden. Touches their flanks whenever they pass, learns the Spanish and Maya-Toltec words for them, feeds them grain, whenever possible, often stolen. He loves them because they accept their reality without words.

In the prints, the animals are chained to bean-filled wagons, ready for export. These he will follow down volcanic pitch, clogged river, to ocean. The wagons idled there, animals allowed only enough rest for the possibility of return.

He will take another photo to show the absence of locomotives, litter the scene with timber, occupy the sea's position so the view is inland, framing pinnacles against talcum-powder thunderheads. Animals unloaded from the metal bellies of ships.

The strand of Central American coastline beneath him, a reminder of bodies.

Silver slide of waves onto the gartered sand: hips against a sacred heat.

10. *Shipping coffee at Champerico*

The *Las Nubes* sequence ends facing the ocean's circular swell, promise of California there in the tide. Every element, moving. A wave cresting in a thick stripe of cream in the photograph's centre. The evolution of landscape.

A small ship is anchored on the beach.

The largest, longest hauling line begins submerged and runs over the boat's hull, across the beach, elevated so it stands about chest high. Five figures are crouched under huge sacks of beans, following it. Their bodies are elbow brackets supporting a vanishing point, successions of waves falling against the anchored keel. (When you look at these backs, you smell salt.)

Two men stand on the boat's prow so, from our perspective, they rise into the water's white anger.

Starting from the bottom left corner, you follow rope to the boat, raise your irises as you read into middle distance, where, left of centre, a packet ship's outline interrupts the air.

The ship, with one stack for steam and a full frontal sail, is the most angular thing Eadweard finds in Central America. Its mast rises with thin diction, disguising engines. The vessel absolutely black against the sea's permanence.

From this dark metal, you slide into sky. Your eye finds stretched steam lifting from the stack. You move right from the left-justified ship, follow grey abstractions to the picture's edge, slide down the outside border to the men bent double under the weight of export. In this way, guiding you, Eadweard solidifies your verbs.

(As you repeat the cycle from men to boats to swells to metal to clouds, the wind in your window translates into waves, splash of language on the page.)

Every bean in the sacks on those backs carrying a memory of music.

ALBUM III:

POSSIBLE

ARRIVALS

RETURNING TO GUATEMALA CITY

1.
Eadweard's first entrance directed by government, he toured the theatre's façade, church bell towers, obliqueness of city streets, and left as fast as he could, politely. Made a beeline towards the densest horizon and disappeared.

Unlike Antigua, no ghosts frequent his photos when he returns here. Instead, Eadweard exposes grand elements of European neoclassicist statuettes. He's careful never to allow more than a few bodies into one shot, assuring a certain abandonment, remembering the green heat of villages. He surrounds humans with columns, sculpture, steeples. Deploys single figures against monolithic cathedrals, legislatures. Slants shoulders against cobblestones.

The walls are armies.

2.
A single figure leans into the national theatre's Parisian stairs as though awaiting execution, sentinel gateways bracketing her possibilities. The Banco Nacional pins two men to its entranceway. A sagging face stuck to a fountain like a white gargoyle. A body decapitated by darkness in a black entranceway to the City Prison. A man's rectangular back against the Economic Society's grand hall, spine a rusted hook. The woman's body seated in front of a Catholic courtyard, holding temples between hands, arched towards the tiled plaza. The sadness in curves.

3.
At the public laundry, Eadweard focuses on space. The building, a giant O, with liquid at its centre, is roofless, contains a sequence of identically arched entranceways. Between each, set in the floor, is a bathtub. Eadweard uses bromide, wanting the tubs bottomless. There's something essential about these empty spaces. Something about the circular tubs echoing the gradual doorways.

4.

Elsewhere, Eadweard wants specificity. He seeks out mortared victims of earthquakes and captures their entropies, naming negatives as though the buildings still stood in perfect order. Roots loop around fissures in the rock, reclaiming minerals. Leaves invade bricks. The dead crosses of the Church of Conception. He places a few remaining walls against air, compares them to the disintegration spread across foregrounds. Scratches his name into lower right corners. Fallen arches, broken bones.

5.

At the cemetery, surrounded by epitaphs, Eadweard creates a new city. Tombs line the walkways like shops. He puts two gigantic people into his metropolis, romanticizing. One standing, back to the lens, hands in pockets, head lifted. The other, sitting to the left by the exterior wall, blending greyness into a collection of mourning. Both figures are irrevocably still. Stuck. The back of the man and the shadows of the sitter. Shut doors.

A plaque is centred on a foregrounded cairn without a cross, surrounded by obsidian. All of its clear letters, in capital type.

It's as though the figures had shuffled past this language, reading, and then paused, understanding in middle distance what their presence meant. The standing man, frozen in knowledge, thinking. The sitting figure staring into a space between itself and tombs. The precise knees. Everything about this scene suggesting permanence.

The plaque's type held up by a parliament of field stones:

CARRERA, it says.

BOARDING AN EXIT: NOVEMBER, 1875

1.

Eadweard slips aboard the ship cloaked in rain.

The weight he transports with him, back to North America, exactly
the same as it had been ten months ago. Only the details shifted.

In Guatemala, three months before departing, he'd watched storms
march into the city, soap walls white, sand down surfaces in washes
of colour. Each afternoon, as the sky sagged, he'd hidden indoors,
thick drops encouraging contrast. When the streets flooded into
rivers, parted by bicycles into two-foot wakes, cockroaches and rats
scurrying up poles, he closed his window, drum of rain a staccato
code across his shaded room. The three peaks above his window,
each named for an element—Volcano Water, Volcano Fire, Volcano
Flower—were a ring around these showers. He relied on them for
heat, a promise of flames against the falling thunder.

When he gets on the steamer in November, he's thinking of this
triad of lava. Pulls out of Central America thinking that rock is an
illusion. That everything, at its heart, is liquid.

On board, he turns away from other passengers, gives them his
back, then hurls it through doorways. (The emulsions, locked in
his trunks below deck, remain there until landing, seventeen days
later, in the city where Flora has died in paralysis, boat coming into
harbour, anchoring.)

En route, he sets his camera against rolling swells, mixes chemistry
in new conditions, degrees. Rain splashes onto his plates, dotting
depictions of ocean with bits of its motion. Eadweard experimenting
with the sea's pitch, trying to freeze it. He twists his head towards
the sterile sun, remembering desert.

In the surviving pictures, you get the deck's ordered boards against the sea's grey anger, forty-five-degree angles to the horizon. Rain is suspended in the air in short, silver ropes.

A triangle rises over the ship's prow, a giant hand strangling metal. Eadweard on the weather deck just then, mixing chemicals, timing the ship's violent collisions into the horizon.

Cold hand reaching into the lens to pluck out his last faith in the beauty of water.

2.

When he arrives in San Francisco, Eadweard heads uphill towards construction, intentional. No one greets him at the dock. The baggage, following him, contains his imagery encased in brown sleeves, red boxes. Husks of flesh around seeds.

On Montgomery Street, he insists that his trunks be left in the hall outside his door. He occupies the room's silence, dust lifting from carpet: Flora, gone. Approaches the flowers, rotted in a yellowed vase on the table. He tips the clear space over the lip of the wood so triangles explode across the floor. Traces a groove through the table's dust to the window's sash, noting how new buildings interrupt old horizon. A continent's edge.

Except for the Guatemala plates and equipment, his luggage is left unopened for a month at the entrance. Instead, he remembers the sleeves of old suits, takes his unexposed album to the Morse Gallery, wanting their truisms hidden.

It's not so much that he wants to forget. He wants their actualities softened by a regulated schedule. Not buried, but blunted. Sleeping in the gallery's archive.

When he speaks to old friends about his trip, he does so always referring to photographs, exchanging chemical compounds for pleasantries. He refers to Guatemala's lush folds as work, presents them as decided spaces. Marks his sequence of coffee beans as popular history, pointing to certain agricultural tools as though referring to moments in an animal's stride: forelegs of planting, leaps of harvest, hyperextensions of beans.

He holds up the quintuplets and slowly names them against the gallery's formality.

But, it's in the final views, the tilt of ocean against his boat's slow path to California, that we get our last views of *Las Nubes*. When you look at the greybeards in the photos, the sky and ocean are mixed with rain, and you can't distinguish them.

What it means to succeed
Or lose.

1876

The Pacific Coast of Central America and Mexico; The Isthmus of Panama; Guatemala; and the Cultivation and Shipment of Coffee.

Illustrated by Muybridge, San Francisco, 1876, the year it had to be.

At the Gallery, he makes five copies of the album, securing Guatemala and the coast between bound boards. They are the most beautiful photographs he has ever made and he wants to burn their perfection.

He spends a week criss-crossing the city, trying to ignore the hills and bay, rubbing against one another in a constant, marginal friction. He gives the albums away to repay debts, wants their grim grace noted and then erased. Arrives at doors of two Napa County lawyers, Silas Selleck, President of the Pacific Mail Steamship Company. In every salon, he talks chemistry and numbers, points to a naked hip in a photo and defines its arithmetic. Details the speed of rivers. Submerges the paper in numbers.

He rides the new streetcar up Clay Street every day, wanting to understand Chinatown, whole city swelling against the bodies there. Machine gliding against the hills, a triumph of steel.

He takes Floredo out of the Catholic orphanage. Holds him as briefly as possible, powder lifting from the child's overalls. He rides the short distance to the Protestant orphanage, plants Floredo there behind an iron fence. Leaves him sitting on the floor of the main room, two years old. Hands the women who will raise him a fist of money and a bank account number. Says nothing.

(Years later, Floredo, having seen two world wars, Depression, becomes a gardener at a stable. With whisky in him, he claims that his father, *Eadweard Muybridge*, gave him a gold pocket watch, wanted him to have its time beside him as he buried his wrists in the compost of opulent backyards. He dies in 1944, a year before Hiroshima burns, an American invention. Skin slipping from hands in clear gloves.)

Eadweard rolls away from the orphanage finalizing his list of social responsibilities, deciding on limits. Distributes the five albums, the boy, and then ignores them. Driven by the year's order. Counting down.

A year later, he climbs Nob Hill to the city's highest structure.

The profile he makes from here, pivoting every fifteen minutes for a new exposure, threads together into a seven-foot strip. 360 degrees of realty, connected by squares. Main roads disappearing towards *the horizon* so that, later, viewers could *orient themselves in the overall scheme of things*. All the rooftops made from trees.

He creates this reality to announce his official entrance into America. The panorama: an exercise in citizenship. His last landscape photographs.

At the time, San Francisco is under curfew. Citizens allowed only one free hour of darkness, secured into homes by ten p.m., released at dawn to seek Chinese shop owners and question their ethics. (Coppinger sleeping, in his suit, on the corners of opium districts, in the street of the gamblers). Alleys are flooded with the US National Guard, sent as a barricade to beatings, guns glinting. The Workingman's Party, unionized, armed. 5438 members of the Committee of Safety, beating anti-Chinese workers to death in the streets, claiming moral victories for the state. Two waves of anger divided by the government's inflexible old-army pistols.

Eadweard reads all this in the newspaper, facts without judgment. This is why, in the panorama, he wants only construction. Why he elongates exposures so that people will collapse more cleanly into blurs.

What's essential here is that Eadweard defines space unilaterally. Tidies a city's incoherent topography. What is essential here is his drift from interior to exterior, and back. Lifting out of floor plans in order to hunt their contours, from above. A harnessing of tides.

(Everything he captures, again, destroyed in less than two decades. San Andreas Fault shaking every spot of time from its ripe, rounded back.)

Evening

It's at the Occidental Hotel bar, cigar smoke rising around bodies like steam, that Eadweard finally stands, politely excuses himself, announcing that he'll return after pissing, carrying an amber shot glass into shadows. Absolutely sober, he drifts to the room's corner and perforates the alley.

Walking the three blocks to the gallery, his feet are drums. When he opens the back door, he closes himself in darkness. He leaves the lights out, having already memorized this space with his hands. The darkroom where he printed the Guatemalans. He runs fingers over countertops, touching bottles. Opens a drawer, scar rubbing against metal handle. He gently stacks the negatives on a table. Places newspapers, in tight balls, around them. From a cabinet, he removes vials of nitric acid and sulphur, sets a clean cotton handkerchief beside his whisky, neatly. He dumps the acids over the table's surface, and wipes them with cloth: the reinvention of gun cotton.

It will be two minutes before the fibres dry, ignite, tipping whisky, lighting paper records. Poised over the makeshift fuse, Eadweard sees Flora, her body, vermilion berries. He runs a litany of images through his mind, tasting. Small things. Perhaps the shape of a particular glacial rock in a bed of stones. What the sunset does to a bowl of apples. The last seconds of *Carrera* leaking out of him into a muted stain across the floorboards. Almost dry. What's essential here is that we don't really know what he's thinking. That his personal movement, the things that made his heart collapse or double, was so veiled that we only get versions of him, partial translations, fragmentary. So, when he sets the fuse across the table, the sureness of the elbow, locked against solidity, everything about him has to be mechanical. The drying sulphur is a complex mathematical proof.

When the gun cotton explodes, the room jumps alive, dragon-tail flames whipping photos. The balls of paper there translate heat into orange flames, already eating into details, flattening women into veils. As the flames spread, bottles corked tidily on shelves, positives hanging from polite lengths of string, the whisky topples, anger spilling out. Eadweard watches the room blaze towards him, smells bromide, iodide, ether, smokeless powder. He sees flames erase unbroken rivers in a two-minute hunger.

When he slips out the door, it is, again, decisive. He pulls a cigar from his jacket, lights it by cupping a match into his scar, holds his head up straight as he re-enters the drunken hotel, through the alley, closing an interior door behind him. Dry.

(The fire that consumes the Morse Gallery destroys every negative Muybridge made in Central America, plus the panorama of San Francisco. Only the albums and early copies of these prints still exist, predicated by heat, recopied with lost contrast into new collotypes. The last years of his language, burnt.)

When he rejoins the Occidental, his sky is cut off by ceiling. Unsupported transit in the wings.

Part Three: Fauna

"Sallie Gardner," owned by Leland Stanford; running at a 1:40 gait over the Palo Alto track, 19th June 1878.

ALBUM I:

PALO
ALTO

Despite what his biographers say
Muybridge's horse was actually broken by four men,
not one.

Its silhouette, captured
at the Palo Alto stock farm,
summer of 1878.

The only time these four bodies
will share the same frame
will be with this background.

Each man's gravity
overlapping,
four names,
four histories:

Stanford,
Isaacs,
Muybridge,
and Charlie Marvin

presented.

2.
First, of course, there was Stanford,
The Governor,
who always wore a vest.

He could push into the smelly scenery of a stable
and transform its acrid shit into something beautiful.
Would extend the arms from his egg-shaped trunk
and collapse them against an animal's flank,
knowing,
by a certain obsession with anatomy,

which muscles would be tensed
according to the idiosyncratic gait of any animal he owned.
Beard around his jaw
a kind of clothing.

Years before,
Stanford had personally built complete sections
of the Southern Pacific,
stitching an iron belt over America's middle.

He claims to have spent nights
stretched on wooden counters
in the high plains,
forgetting to start fires
so his moustache met mornings coated in frost,
shoulders echoing the snow-capped Rockies.

When he meets the eastern line in Ogden,
1869,
he centres himself in images,
silver spikes beneath his shoe soles only later
replaced by regulation iron.

Talking about those early days,
he always mentions how he and Jane,
Mrs. Governor,
built their furniture from dry-goods boxes and boards.
How they'd scrubbed the cheap grain as though it were gold,
channelled their shoulders into wood
and prayed for sanitation.

That he believed so hard for so long
that the furniture was rosewood
with silver inlay,
it transformed into riches.

Says that
that wood was what [he] knew best in this world,
that
nothing compares to using your own hammer
with your own hands.

Presents the palms to crowds, displaying calluses.

Now,
nearly a decade later,
he's returned to his supposed roots:
the farm.

When Stanford builds Palo Alto,
he believes in abolition so vehemently
that he extends humanity to certain animals.

In the stables, rules are stringent,
designed by Stanford himself,
horse homes
as quiet and orderly as a church.
Loud talking, swearing, harsh language, scolding,
and whipping are not allowed.
Posted about the stables are rules
forbidding these practices.
Anyone breaking any rule is dismissed.

Horses are taught as prized children,
given lush beds by altruistic master craftsmen,
equestrian coats brushed in seductive strokes,
as though the humans were in love.

Mares receive complete sides of conversations
by handlers who read responses
by the precise positions of legs, ears,
confiding, as though to spouses,
their secrets,

accepting simple readjustments
of an animal's withers
as wisdom.

The best sires receive the same affection
as retired swayback mares, who,
put out to pasture,
are kept peaceful into old age,
dying in luxurious pillows of straw
with specially prepared diets
of steamed gourmet grains.

No animal is ever killed on the farm
except out of pity.
Age, sex and colour
are not considerations.
An equine democracy.
A political multiculture of beasts.

This way, in his frequent absences,
every member of the farm becomes a version
of Stanford's intuition.
Any person entering homes, tools, schedules,
is aware that Stanford is there.
Stepping into doorways means inhabiting his suits,
structures fitting around lives like loose linen.

Even upon his first arrival, Eadweard understood this.

In the animals' folds,
he could allow technology without contradiction,
could accept the constructions all across the farm
as nourishment.
He ran his English hand across a horse's crest
and knew why American machines
were going to be used to track its speed,
why the continent's unbroken wilderness
had been spanned by Stanford's careful iron,

why acids run across a photographic plate
had to be manipulated.

He pushed so hard into the farm's details
that the whole direction of the place seemed built
into every fibre.
That here, finally, was a landscape where
focus and detail were as important as narrative.
That a full story could be gleaned in any leaf,
any leg of any animal.
Symbolism of the farm and the state and the country
summarized
by one exact placement of a coronet.
That he was ingesting genealogies.
The buildings against the animals: a civilization.

As Charlie tells him the day Eadweard arrives,
Everyone is first a citizen of the farm,
then an American.

3.
Muybridge, the second man,
arrives in spring.

He's convinced the Governor to finance experiments
in quick-shutter chronophotography
packed up practical tools and minimal clothing
from the Montgomery Street place
and shipped them here.
(When he lists the apartment for sale in the *Post*,
the advertisement includes all of his furniture,
even those flowers drying on the floor in their jigsaw of glass.)

He arrives in Stanford's absence,
his introduction to the farm, unofficial.

He's met by the only other person
who wakes up before dawn,
to feed, scrub, ride, study:
the equerry, Charles Marvin.

The third man: Charlie.

When he canters up to Eadweard
wearing terracotta jodhpurs,
Charlie digs a heel into the dirt, caracoling,
and trots off to Eadweard's new house,
away from Stanford's mansion,
towards the stables, towards light.

Charlie's voice is deep,
and he talks the entire time
they weave through property,
mapping.

He uses complete sentences to describe
paddocks, stalls, stables.
Gives every animal a proper name and a paragraph.

Each building based in human technology
gets a two-syllable label instead:
black-smith, wheel-wright, feed-mill, bar-ber, laun-dry.

By the time they reach the dusty little room
where Eadweard will spend most of the next two years,
Charlie's outlined the whole society of the ranch,
all 150 souls at least gestured to,
horses, capitalized.

Says, as we already know, that
This is the Governor's world. Remember that.

When he hands Eadweard his hackneyed suitcases,
having carried them,
two cups of coffee, a brush, and a pocket watch
with absolute balance,

not spilling a drop, he says
Here it is, I believe. The camera shed beside you.
And then, meeting his eye for the first time,
stretches his arms as wide as he can,
rearing slightly so his toes levitate.

This is where Electioneer used to feed, he says.
The best damned stallion in the world, and I know it!

He folds in his wingspan
to take Eadweard's scar into his paw:
Charles Marvin. I'm the trainer.
You treat them phillies right, and we'll be fine.

Every record-breaking Stanford horse the farm produces
will be broken, trained, jockeyed
and encouraged by this man.
Eadweard will never find out where he came from
or where he ends up.
Charlie being defined, always,
by a certain way of walking,
a way of breathing into a stallion's ear,
covering his speech with a thick wrist
so no one could invade that privacy.

What's important here, only, is presence,
is how Charlie steers Muybridge
into the history of motion.

On that first day, he leaves Eadweard alone,
leather handle of his case
already feeling wrong.

The thickness of hide in his fist:

a thoroughbred's ankle.

4.
Three months later.

The camera shed is one hundred feet long, nine high,
perched along a racetrack,
empty slot centred
on the shed's west side, waist high,
numbers *1* to *12*
in two-foot intervals
above it,
one label for each stereoscope.

Eadweard's house is twenty feet from here,
shadow of one building just reaching the other
in mid-morning.

He shifts his weight from shack to shed,
wanting things proven,

carries a rectangular mirror inside,
interrupting darkness
in a yellow avenue of details.

The shed,
already stocked
with corked bottles,
with shelves of glass,
polished and stacked,

ready for an afternoon's
circuitry.

5.
With electricity,
we're introduced to the fourth man:
John Isaacs, engineer.

He's the final, formulaic corner.
The composition's balance.
Without him, the horse would slip
out of its frames
and blur.

Although he arrives that morning
straight from desert,
where he's slept for a week,
the folds of his jacket carry
only the slightest hints of sand.

He is the tidiest person Eadweard's met,
hair cropped close,
brown eyes alert
behind thinly rimmed spectacles,
moustache trimmed to echo the circumference of lips.
His suits are always faultlessly creased,
metallic.
Ivory collar against tan.

Working on Stanford's rail routes,
Isaacs made his reputation for inventions.

He approached mountains holding hands out
to avalanches, feeling density.
Could spend an hour on an outcrop
and emerge with a blueprint
for a decade of tracks,
path of least resistance marked
on a makeshift map,
to scale,
only words given to his foreman
a series of numbers.

150

He electrifies landscapes,
nets and channels blue fire.
Is able to see pure physics,
to watch the pathway of a boulder
down a slope
and know the number of leaps it needs
to reach sea level.
He spends unedited weeks outdoors
during construction,
sleeping under firs,
through thunderstorms,
and never gets dirty.

Could wear the same shirt for a month
without sweating,
without stains.

Every angle in him
crisply calculated.

What Eadweard respects most about him
is that he offers only the bare minimum
of language,
the most intimate sentence
he's ever heard him say being,

What I like best
about numbers
is that they're always
in capital
type.

Square jaw working
around the words.

6.

When Eadweard approaches him that morning,
Isaacs is already on the track,
evaluating.

He crouches to the lime-coated dirt,
nods,
white index finger on his chin.

Behind him, Eadweard:
Hello Mr. Isaacs.

Without turning, he nods,
says,
Eadweard,
one hand aloft,
offering a scribbled diagram,
still staring at the bevelled wall
opposite the cameras.

As Eadweard reads the paper,
John brings two lengths of wood onto the soil,
places them exactly parallel
in a channel.
Says,
The left sulky wheel,
and then, turning,
smiles,
having solved the problem
of automated electrical shutters,
A sight for Charlie.

Moves several feet back
from the target,
nods again,
proofing.

Muybridge kneeling beside the two planks,
constructing
lines.

7.

Two days later, all four men are finally here:
Eadweard, Leland, John and Charlie.

June 19th, 1878.

Stanford has invited California's newspapers.

It's rumoured he's bet businessmen
a thousand dollars each
that his horse, *Occident*, will have
all its hooves off the ground
during its gait.

The money reported in every West Coast daily,
a month of speculation preceding this morning's exposures.

Stanford waits until noon to take advantage of the best light,
reporters queued behind the track's white rail.

John points towards lime, recites numbers.

For each camera, he explains,
an electrical wire is buried,
so that a cart's wheel will depress it,
triggering switches in all twelve shutters.

He says *Occident* will be rushing past them
at more than forty feet a second,
that the circuitry will be invisible,
that all the shutters will seem to go off
at once.

In the studio,
eleven mechanisms already loaded,
Eadweard pours collodion over the final plate,
dips into nitrate,
acids curling into air, room silent.
He lifts his preparations by a corner
and slots them into the twelfth camera.

There is brief applause as Stanford winks
and vacates the racing surface.

Half a track away, Charlie hops into the sulky.

At Isaacs' signal,
Occident rounds the corner
towards the straightaway
where we're waiting,

Eadweard in the shed, face between numbers.

Hooves along the track, gaining volume.
Charlie, a black silhouette,
dirt flying in sequences of four
as he approaches the crowd,
left wheel of the cart bearing down on John's sight,
Stanford holding his watch.

When they arrive at the studio installation,
external sound disappears.
There is only the rhythm of the hooves,
blurred legs,
Charlie's hand gently curving through air,
animal's tail trailing behind him
in a slipstream whisper.
When the wheel enters his sight,
Muybridge holds his breath.

In two-thirds of a second, the shutters rattle into life,
their sights crossing in front of lenses,
zapping plates with yellow bursts
that explode in the shed like bullets,
cart wheeling down the track
as Eadweard hears the muffled cheers of newsmen,
Stanford uncorking champagne and distributing goblets,
pouring glass after glass of bronze confidence.

In the shed, Eadweard works frantically
to get all twenty-four horses out of the cameras.

He takes up his station by the water tank
where six pairs are fixed, rinsed,
set on a double shelf beneath corresponding numbers,
frozen soil spread across the negative's bottoms,
wingspans.

When he sees the seventh frame,
he removes his cameras from their perches,
so a banner of light draws a thick highlight
across the room.

He replaces acid trays under countertops,
recorks bottles,
wipes hands with towels,
invites the crowd into the one-hundred-foot hallway,
asking everyone to slip
into glass.

In the seventh frame,
a wingless horse hovers half a foot above the earth.

Stanford, beside him,
shakes his hand with such force
that Eadweard bends double.

The Governor's faith proven
with several dozen witnesses,
reputation confirmed,
horsesense undeniable.

The reporters shout at the truth of sunlight,
applauding around notebooks.

Every equestrian painting disproved
with half an hour of machinery.

8.

This is how, at forty-eight, Eadweard becomes
the man who seems in retrospect
like a bullet shot through a book;

His trajectory ripped through
all the central stories of his time...

the man who split
the second,
as dramatic
and far-reaching
as the splitting
of the atom.

9.
Hours later,
Muybridge, Isaacs and Stanford
having retired
to the mansion,
the racetrack is mute
under high trees.

Left alone,
Charlie sidles into the shed
where the pictures are.

He arcs into his own image,
nose against silhouette,
and shakes his head.

Not in disbelief,
but in the miracle of translation.

He passades a step,
runs his eyes across
the shed's conformation,
aims fingers out the door,
over fields.

As he turns his back
to the cameras,
definitively,
he's already edging
towards horses,

their muscles,
a reminder of earth.

Pegasus,
he says.

ALBUM II:

PROOF

1.
By next summer,
Muybridge's horse is copied onto woodcuts,
printed on the cover of *Scientific American.*

People arrive at the farm for interviews,
creep around Eadweard's little shack,
opening books, tapping teacups,
wanting to measure the exact circumference of biceps,
length of his beard.

Muybridge gives them dopey grins,
tumblers of clouded water.
When they ask long, convoluted questions
detailing the veterinary history of equine locomotion,
Eadweard says,
Maybe.

2.
There are details here. Be patient.
The right metal can open any lock.
Each lens is a circle.
Every image squared.

3.
People send hate mail, publish angry cartoons,
splayfoot horses contorted, caricatures.

Newspapers reprint famous equine sculptures, paintings.
Enraged columnists dismiss electricity.
Artists actually shake with anger,
refusing to surrender the meanders they believe in.
Auguste Rodin, thinking,
It is the artist who is truthful and it is photography which lies
for in reality time does not stop!

4.
There are patient details here.
This is what's left over from debate, invention.
how *terra nullis* grows
rivers.

5.

Eadweard plans a summer zoology:
The backs of elephants, a dog's stride.

A single wire ignites each forty-eight-shutter explosion
for the particular gaits of hogs, deer, dogs, oxen, bulls,
circus horses in various leaps, jumps, whinnies, kicks.

Assistants slap caged flanks, prod bodies,
have to try at least a dozen times
before each beast will trot across the angry shutters.

In July, they secure a sequence of wings,
clatter startling bodies,
the continental birds coming out indistinct,
cloudy outlines defying everything they're doing.

6.

How Eadweard's detailing means, eventually
that his animals will be permanently shelved
in the veterinary stacks.
Shifted from art into scientific Darwinism.
The subtext of call numbers.

7.

In August, athletes from the Olympic Club:
Eadweard's first humans.

One sequence details a gymnast's backflip,
acute body contorted
hovering
horizontal
aiming its head at horizons,
land bookending his spin.

Eadweard mounts him on the studio wall, inverting.

8.

How to sketch the right angles into history.
How archived photographs are held
with white gloves and proper identification.
The vaults where the most valuable clues are locked up.
The official appointments needed to make claims on
what we've lost.

9.

Before showcasing his results,
Muybridge dodges and burns.

He holds up twenty-four frames
of a running dog,
against a window,
thumbing corners:
zoetrope.

Animal trotting in his hand's scar,
a viewfinder.

10.
Less a chronology than an attitude, then.
Less reproduction than mathematics.
Be patient.
The more specific you are,
the more general it will be.

11.
By 1881, Palo Alto's repetition
seeps into Eadweard's San Francisco
routine.

Every movement he makes is a lost moment.

He confuses pedestrians
with subjects,
negotiates streets
by separating people's legs
into phases.

Spends his summers killing clocks.

Stanford,
Isaacs
and Charlie
against his minute hands.

12.
How to measure,
to reproduce, reduce, assemble,
an archive's connections.

How to ground your theories,
to figure ground,
to find common ground
in your selection of images.

162

Each stanza,
naming.

(There are details, here.
Be patient.
Meander if you want to get to town.)

13.
Eventually, in Stanford's living room,
Eadweard's invention is hidden,
afternoon blocked out with thick cotton curtains.

This is Eadweard's proudest technology.
He hides it for protection.
Calls it, reverently,
zoopraxiscope.

He sets the Stanford family's chairs in a semicircle
facing a blank, stretched canvas,
and asks the group, smiling,
to please keep their eyes forward,
slips to the rear, unveiling.
Flips an electric switch.

Two discs begin spinning,
one with images drawn on edges,
the other a series of windows,
projections leaking from the intersections.
Removing his hat from the lens,
a life-sized horse leaps onto the wall.

Mrs. Stanford, standing,
spills tea across her yellow dress.
Leland Junior staring
like those newspapermen had two years ago.
Stanford sitting there like a boulder.

Horse trotting across the casual, muted screen: cinema.

ALBUM III:

THREE
COUNTRIES

1.

With Stanford touring India, things get bad:
Muybridge's horse against the Governor's *Horse in Motion*,
the imagery published as woodcuts,
no mention of Eadweard in the whole volume.

Eadweard declares *rights*,
and, within a year, loses.

The Governor at the trial, calling the judge by name.
Isaacs, not meeting Eadweard's eye, saying,
Chemistry takes second place to Stanford's ideology.

Eadweard keeps his focus by thinking numbers:
Judge's hammer in twelve phases against oak.
He has to concentrate on such dissections to stay alert.
Clouds of powder infesting the courtroom.

Proof against belief.

2.

In Marey's living room,
Meissonier hosts Muybridge's introduction to France,
by taking a vow never to paint a horse again,
an extremity Eadweard finds quite admirable.

Two hundred Parisians leaning into the translation,
erupting in hands.

3.
In England,
Eadweard finds himself
surrounded by so many borders
that maps no longer matter.

When he speaks at the Royal Institution,
Duke of Edinburgh, Prince and Princess of Wales,
Alfred, Lord Tennyson watching him
rewrite the charge of the light brigade,
jewelled bodies project split illuminations.

The Prince requests boxing,
and Eadweard spins into response, bowing.

The two men he throws onto the screen pound one another,
faces contorted, hurtled
into boulders.

ALBUM IV:

PENNSYLVANIA:
MAN
ASCENDING
AN
INCLINE

1.

Muybridge officially moves east
the year Leland Stanford Junior dies
in a Naples hospital,
Jane's back crooked over the bed.

Stanford dedicates a university, inspired by angels.
Money versus memory.

(Floredo still planted in that San Francisco orphanage.)

2.

Plate 470: Child running after a man. Males and Females (DRAPED)

3.
What he's famous for.

At the University of Philadelphia,
Eadweard takes two years to paralyze
twenty-five thousand images of bodies
and arrange them in a ten-volume book:
Human and Animal Locomotion.

All the sequences are backgrounded
by a network of exact, Cartesian coordinates,
white strings stretched taut into two-inch squares,
a triad of cameras for every thousandth of a second.

He carries his portable technology
to tracks, zoos, hospitals,
hunting.
With the invention of celluloid, he minimizes his use of glass,
sand reminding him of beaches, coasts.

He caps the last of his bottles,
orders a whole crate of the new "lightning"
quick dry plates,
manufactured, ready to use,
twenty times more sensitive than his own manipulations were,
less than a decade before.

Last collodion left by the Pacific, sinking.

4.

32: *Walking and carrying a bucket of water in each hand.*
Females (NUDE)

42: *Walking and pouring water from a pitcher.* Females (NUDE)

43: *Walking, sprinkling water from a basin and turning around.*
Females (NUDE)

51: *Walking, turning around and using a sprinkling pot.*
Females (NUDE)

81: *Ascending an incline with a bucket of water in each hand.*
Females (NUDE)

102: *Turning and ascending stairs with a bucket of water.*
Females (NUDE)

120: *Descending an incline with a bucket of water in right hand.*
Females (NUDE)

147: *Descending stairs and turning with a water jar on shoulder.*
Females (NUDE)

175: *Crossing brook on stepping-stones with fishing pole and basket.*
Females (NUDE)

203: *Bending over a trestle with a water jar.* Females (NUDE)

222: *Stooping, lifting a water jar to head and turning.* Females (NUDE)

225: *Removing a water jar from shoulder to the ground.*
Females (NUDE)

228: *Turning and lifting a water jar from the ground.* Females (NUDE)

234: *Lifting and emptying a basin of water and turning.*
Females (NUDE)

244: *Sitting, crossing legs and filling a goblet from a pitcher.*
Females (NUDE)

401: Emptying a bucket of water. Females (NUDE)

402: Emptying a basin of water. Females (NUDE)

406–408: Woman pouring a bucket of water over another woman. Females (NUDE)

409: Pouring a basin of water over head. Females (NUDE)

410: Stepping out of bathtub, sitting and wiping feet. Females (NUDE)

411: Lifting a towel while sitting and wiping feet. Females (NUDE)

412: Washing, wiping face and turning. Females (NUDE)

413: Pouring water in basin and washing face. Females (NUDE)

414: Wiping body with towel. Females (NUDE)

432: Washing clothes at a tub. Females (NUDE)

433: Wringing clothes. Females (NUDE)

440: Stooping and rinsing a tumbler. Females (NUDE)

441: Carrying a vase and placing it on a table. Females (NUDE)

443: Drinking from a goblet while standing. Females (NUDE)

445: Woman drinking from water jar on shoulder of another woman. Females (NUDE)

446: Filling a pitcher on the ground from a water jar. Females (NUDE)

500: Various movements with a water jug. Females (NUDE)

516: Miscellaneous movements with a water jar. Females (NUDE)

462: Pouring a libation on the ground and drinking from a goblet. Females. (TRANSPARENT DRAPERY)

5.
Weight bearing.

A dozen horses, two mules, a goat
straining against ropes,
human bodies braced diagonal,
leading.
Carts strapped to quadruped backs.

Men lift colossal boulders across the white grids,
launching ashen shadows into middle distance.
Triggering.

A legless amputee swinging himself,
torso hinged against the lowest white lines.

The 340-pound woman whom Eadweard describes
as *20, unmarried,*
urging her body up.

Females (NUDES).
Except as noted:

182: Crawling on hands and knees.

219: Stooping, lifting a broom and sweeping.

252: Kneeling on right knee and scrubbing the floor.

264: Getting out of bed and preparing to kneel.

432: Washing clothes at a tub.

433: Wringing clothes.

435: Ironing clothes.

436: Making up a bed.

437: Setting down a bucket and preparing to sweep (DRAPED)

437: Setting down a bucket and preparing to scrub (DRAPED)

528: A-C: Carrying a child.

Males (NUDES).
Except as noted:

376: Blacksmith, hammering an anvil with two hands.

379: Carpenter, planing. (PELVIS CLOTH)

381. Mason, laying. (PELVIS CLOTH)

385: Farmer, using a pick.

386: Miner, using a pick (DRAPED)

387: Farmer, using a long-handled shovel.

388: Farmer, using a spade.

389: Farmer, scattering seed.

390: Farmer, mowing grass.

392: Dragging a garden roller.

394: Turning a crank handle.

396: Pounding with a mallet.

508: Shoeing a horse.

7.

Eadweard personally fires the new shutters,
but passes all twenty-five thousand exposures
to student assistants,
pointing vaguely to trays of acid,
wanting no part of submersion.

Paper proofs are printed in cyan monotones,
numbers scratched over a string orchestra.
Originals ordered, selections set onto singular strips of celluloid.

He slips from first to third person with unconscious electricity.
The eye, shifted.

Eadweard insists on his archive of limbs so much,
the detailed positions of explicit bones,
that, looking at the sequences,
you lose specificity, geography, reference, historical time,
emerge from *Animal Locomotion* as though it were one image,
repeated.
All 781 variations bound with paused thread.

8.
When you look at these pictures, you witness fictions:

Plate 541. Artificially induced convulsions, while sitting.
A prostitute recruited from San Francisco.
Eadweard pays her ten dollars to receive electric shocks,
hooks wires to her thighs, hides behind viewfinders.
Her hands still shake after the Gatling gun of shutters explodes.

Plate 527. A-C: Spanking a child.
A naked woman sitting on the ground.
Eadweard directs her hand down towards a child's buttocks,
surrounds the scene with lenses.
The woman never makes contact,
leaves the child hanging there, facing us.
Eadweard refusing to create the reality he wanted.

Nude descending a staircase.
Duchamp's brush, painting.
Triangles of white oil that are Eadweard's beard
in a diagonal descent to the Pennsylvania horizon.
Repeating.

9.
During the two years he spends working at the University,
Eadweard wears the same clothes every day,
seams opening.

He continually carries a sack of lemons.
Combines citric acid and large slabs of white cheese
with maggots in the holes.
Calls his lunches "cheesegerms"
and gulps their activity like medicine.

He lets his beard grow long enough, cleans it seldom enough,
that its middle section is stained brown
from repeated pipe tobacco.

At least once a week a child rushes up to him:
white hair, beard, unplumbed blushes
emerging from ample cheekbones;
each small body's quick intelligence
mistaking him for an uncanny Santa Claus.

10.
Plate 519: A: Throwing a disk. B: Ascending a step. C: Walking.
An ex-athlete.
Showing the assistants that nudity was necessary,
Eadweard climbs the stairs
so his penis flops upwards, out from the body.
fifty-four years old and the sturdy stomach
without even a slight bulge.
His face, a white explosion. A Greek legend.

11.
Summoned to the Dean's office,
several months into shooting,
Eadweard is told, sternly,
to look after appearances,
curls poking out of his hat in a flame.

He removes the brim from his forehead,
hair slipping out of its socket, says,
What do you mean, Sir?
Holds the hat an inch from his nose,
seeing it for the first time.

Then, loudly: *Why, there is a hole in it!*

When he puts a finger through the lost material,
his stained nail emerges from the hollow.
Bag of citrus on his thigh.

12.

Plates 537-541 and *546-562.* (Patients from Blockley Hospital)
ABNORMAL MOVEMENTS: MALES & FEMALES
(NUDE & SEMI-NUDE)

537: Single amputation of leg, hopping with crutches.
538: Double amputation of legs, boy.
539: Infantile paralysis, child walking on hands and feet.
540: A: Bowlegs, boy. B: Spinal caries, girl walking.
541 and 553: Spastic walking.
547: Spastic, walking with a crutch.
552: Spastic walking with cane.
548: Lateral sclerosis, walking.
546, 549, 554. 560: Locomotor ataxia, walking.
550: Locomotor ataxia, walking. A: Arms up. B: Arms down.
551: Epilepsy, walking.
556: Local chorea, lying down.
557: Local chorea, standing.
555: Muscular atrophy of legs, adult, walking.
558: Stuporous melancholia, walking.
559: Partial paraplegia, walking with cane.
561: Hydrocephalus, walking.
562: Lateral curvature of spine, walking.

Eadweard, *the living photographer, behind the emotionless lens.*

13.

Plate 365. Head-spring, a flying pigeon interfering. Males (NUDE)

14.
Eadweard targets the birds for a whole month.

He deposits pigeons in a wicker box, cocked,
places it at one extremity of the grid.

With a signal, he unfastens the lid, a sight.

Most of the animals wait long enough to escape without record,
refusing flight.
Others, immediate bullets, desperate for air,
lift so quickly that Eadweard has thirty empty plates
and six pictures of dove claws.

At the zoo, he dips into exotica.
Cockatoo, American bald eagle, Quetzal,
chronicled on celluloid.

What he doesn't tell his audiences, lecturing, later,
pointing at the famous feathers
that spoon through the air like oars,
is that every bird he photographs is tied down by an ankle.

The animal, released from its cage, thin rope uncoiling,
nearly invisible against background.
He lets feathers taste the air beyond enclosures,
lets them slip out of discipline as the final lengths of cord unwind.
Beaks turning towards relief in every sequence of the book.

Moments later, ropes are obvious,
lines across gelatin,
bodies fracturing the air
just as the shutters stop rattling.

Eadweard wanting the snaps audible
so he knew they were completed.

15.

Plate 723. Lion walking and turning around.

At the zoo, they separate George from his mate,
drop a white backdrop screen over the door in his enclosure,
trapping him, bar shadows striping.
They poke him in the ribs with a stick until he screams,
tears into the background,
moving as far as he can from cameras.

The heat in Panama.

16.

Females (NUDE):

444: Two women shaking hands and kissing each other.

*54: Two women walking arm in arm and turning around;
one flirting a fan.*

196: Two women dancing a waltz.

239: One woman standing, another sitting and crossing legs.

245: Two women turning around and sitting on the ground.

427–429: Woman disrobing another.

444: Two women shaking hands and kissing each other.

*448: Woman descending stairs with a goblet
meets another woman with a bouquet.*

*450: Woman brings a cup of tea;
another woman takes the cup and drinks.*

*452: Woman kneels and drinks from the water jar of another woman
and both walk off.*

464: Woman chasing another woman with a broom.
Females (DRAPED)

17.
Plates 351–361 are men, in loincloths,
displaying arms, charging with bayonets,
wedged against soil, firing rifles.

In any sequence where two men face one another,
they simulate war.
Boxing, open-handed, dark bruises across hard cheeks.
Plate 341: Striking a blow with left hand.
Plate 344: Striking a blow with right hand.
Plate 333: Boxing, one man knocking the other one down.
Bones crushed beneath bodies.

18.
Plate 66. Running.

Charles Leonard, a radiology pioneer at the university.
A nude study. A true story.

He is exposing the skin, thinking.
The portrait inverting the doctor's work,
stitching rays through the muscular system,
finding the invisible recesses of bodies on gelatin.
The spectacles and moustache.

This profile is taken only months after his wife dies
from overexposure to x-ray radiation.
The necklace slipping over his back shaped exactly like a noose.

19

22: Walking with high-heeled boots on. Females (NUDE)

142: Descending stairs and turning, dress caught. Females (DRAPED)

202: Dropping and lifting a handkerchief. Females (NUDE)

207: Stooping and lifting train. Females (DRAPED)

367: Kicking a hat. Females (NUDE)

415: Toilet, preparing to put on clothing. Females (NUDE)

416: Toilet, putting on dress. Females (NUDE)

418: Toilet, sitting and putting on stockings. Females (NUDE)

425: Toilet, putting on dress and turning around. Females (NUDE)

426: Toilet, brushing hair and walking off. Females (NUDE)

430: Taking off clothing. Females (NUDE)

432: Washing clothes at a tub. Females (NUDE)

433: Wringing clothes. Females (NUDE)

434: Hanging clothes on a line. Females (NUDE)

435: Ironing clothes. Females (NUDE)

461: Opening a parasol and turning around. Females (SEMI-NUDE)

20.

Plate 187. Dancing (fancy). Photo 11 (Pirouette.)
A lantern slide Eadweard bequeaths to the town of Kingston.
A transparent dress.

Eadweard made over a thousand of these,
asking young women to act,
to offer their bodies to machinery
and let him enter them, framing.

They look at us and smile.

Here, a body, paused in a spiral,
holds cloth up to a waist, hand cresting hips,
head tilted to Eadweard, behind the lens.

His fingerprint on the cheek's curvature, where it disintegrates.

21.

Plate 441: Carrying a vase and placing it on a table. Females (NUDE)

22.

In 1891, after fourteen years on Stanford's farm,
Eadweard selling collections across the sorrel British Isles,
Charles Marvin leaves Palo Alto without explanation,
packs a bag and disappears, a green jumper.
(Stanford dying two years later, thirteen years before Jane.)

Charlie eventually ends up in Pennsylvania, a dobbin.
Dies in pasture.

Muybridge, seven years before,
photographing in Philadelphia, thinking of him,
named every horse as though human,
touched stars, medicine hats, offering apples,
secured his battery of cameras thinking
of high trees.

23.

A thousand photographs of horses.

24.

1904 and Eadweard has moved permanently back to England.

After Pennsylvania, he never photographs professionally again.
Spends two decades concentrating on bodies, cycling.

He returns to a heritage home in Kingston,
minutes from his childhood.
Settles himself by a routine river.

(Edison claims the invention of movies that decade,
puts reels of film into little booths
that let you see ten seconds of action
for a nickel,
lengths of celluloid that would've needed sixteen thousand
Muybridge stills to be produced.
Movie business already killing theatre.
Realism of bodies on the larger-than-life screens,
more believable than actors.)

Eadweard's stroke, that year,
while building a scale model of the Great Lakes,
liquid convolutions guided into peat moss.

He slumps over a shovel, mouth adrift,
pipe descending in a single spin
to the flowerbed, forehead finding
the borders of Lake Ontario.

His body. Fresh water.

Epilogue

BOARDING AN EXIT: 1906

1.
The earth reacts against architecture,
disconnecting San Francisco.

Streets halting at new canyons
in intersections.

When the earthquake strikes at five a.m.,
the city vibrates for four minutes,

walls collapsing around
bodies asleep in beds,

bits of foundation leaping out of floors
into ceilings.

The new electric lights at the *Chronicle* building
shatter into triangles.

Every utility source coming into the city
blocked by fragments,

nutrients choked by fire, morning lit by natural flames
on burning corpses.

Every bridge stretching across the bay
collapses.

2.
The *Evening Daily News.* April 18, 1906:

The surgeons moved to the Mechanics' Pavilion, which today is a combined hospital and morgue. Dead and dying are brought in by autos, ambulances, and even garbage carts. Insane patients are taken from the Emergency Hospital. Many of them are hurt. Some break loose and run among the dying, adding horror to the scene.

Fifty thousand homeless bodies flooding the streets, city on fire all day.

The next morning, the fire department charts flames, tracks them on maps, stalking. They anticipate heat, wind, lace homes in the orange path of inertia with dynamite, wanting to halt emperature. China cabinets flying into streets, silver platters suspended in the air. Linen closets excommunicated from interiors. A pedestal toilet sinking in Montgomery Street. The Grand Opera House exposing its skeleton. The *Post* erased within minutes, editorial departments eaten.

When martial law is declared, politicians huddling under half-fallen roofs, planning policy, City Hall *a complete wreck*, the National Guard aims its rifles at nine looters, erasing them from history. Bullets dismantling the plumage of rib cages.

(Every address Eadweard had in San Francisco burns.)

3.
Less than a year later, Alcatraz is a prison:

part 1: green slope of earth against brick-red sky

part 2: the bay's welcome blue

part 3: this city's crumpled geometry,
blistered by yellow tongues

(three versions of a coastline)

SOURCES

*I'm indebted to several biographical and scientific accounts of Eadweard's life, career and age: Robert Bartlett Haas's *Muybridge: Man in Motion*; Robert Mayer's *San Francisco: A Chronological & Documentary History, 1542–1970*; Gordon Hendricks' *Eadweard Muybridge: The Father of the Motion Picture*; Mark Pendergrast's *Uncommon Grounds: The History of Coffee and How It Transformed Our World*, Norman E. Tutorow's *Leland Stanford: Man of Many Careers*; Beaumont Newhall's *History of Photography from 1839 to the Present Day*; Hollis Frampton's short essay "Eadweard Muybridge: Fragments of a Tesseract"; Robert Van Pelt's *Forest Giants of the Pacific Coast*; and E. Bradford Burns exceptional book *Eadweard Muybridge In Guatemala: The Photographer as Social Recorder*. Newspapers, bulletins, and journals from the day have also been invaluable. Quotations from these and other sources appear in italics throughout the poems.

* My epigraphs come from Roland Barthes' *Camera Lucida: Reflections on Photography* (New York: Hill and Wang, 1981. 95–6), lines from which are repeated in "Translating a Map of Guatemala, 1875"; Michael Ondaajte's *In the Skin of a Lion* (Toronto: McClelland & Stewart, 1987. 146), the last line of which is repeated in "Album 2: Proof"; and Susan Sontag's *On Photography* (New York: Farrar, Strauss, and Giroux, 1977. 24.).

* The chemistry described in "Liquid Light" has been gleaned from Newhall's *The History of Photography from 1839 to the Present Day*. (4th ed. New York: Museum of Modern Art, 1964. 47–48). "Liquid Light" is a cheap, contemporary variation of traditional collodion.

*Haas's biography, Muybridge: Man in Motion (Berkeley: U of California, 1976), led me to many of the newspaper sources that told Eadweard's, Flora's and Harry's stories, and was an inspiration for Part One. Italicized lines in the poems are quoted from Hass in "Fixing the River" (3; 40), in "Contemplation Rock" (74–6), at the end of section 12 in "Album 4: Pennsylvania: Man Ascending an Incline" (203), and altered for both the long section detailing the murder in "Arriving at Vallejo" (68), and the exchange of words between Harry and Eadweard that precedes it. Some of the dialogue presented in "Plot and Melodrama" is from Haas's use of California newspaper articles reporting on Muybridge's trial (65–67)

*A line from Mary Louise Pratt's *Imperial Eyes: Travel Writing and Transculturation* (New York: Routledge, 1992. 208) appears in section 1 of "Overland Express, or, the Birth of Helios."

* Robert Van Pelt's entry on "General Sherman" in Forest Giants of the Pacific Coast (Seattle: University of Washington, 2001. 5) provides a line to describe Yosemite's Mammoth Trees in section 2 of "Photograph of Eadweard Pretending to Slip from a Yosemite Valley Mountain".

*Muybridge announced his photographs of "Blossom Rock" in Anthony's Photographic Bulletin, September 1878. A line from his description appears near the beginning of the poem.

*Frampton's essay, "Fragments of a Tesseract" (Circles of Confusion: film, photography, video: texts 1968–1980. Rochester (NY): Visual Studies Workshop, 1983. 79) provides the phrase "man raising a pistol and firing" in "Arriving at Vallejo".

* Descriptions of Larkyns given in "Suits" are taken from Harry's eulogy, delivered by his friend, Harry Edwards, and included in his book of memoirs *A Mingled Yarn* (New York: Putnam, 1883. 152–154).

* The doctor's voice in "Verdict" is taken from newspaper reportage quoted in Hendricks' *Eadweard Muybridge: The Father of the Motion Picture* (New York: Grossman, 1975. 77).

* Many titles and subtitles in Part Two (including those in "Las Nubes") are taken verbatim from Eadweard's surviving Central

American plates in his 1876 album. Errors in translation, labelling and spelling are his, not mine.

* Information about coffee production in "Las Nubes" was informed, in part, by Pendergrast's *Uncommon Grounds: The History of Coffee and How It Transformed Our World* (New York: Basic, 1999). The line on "Indians" as "children", given by Willie Nelson in the subsection "another bean history", is, according to Pendergrast, attributed to Erwin Paul Dieselfdorff, a German finca owner in Guatemala in the late 1870s (36). Other lines from Pendergrast appear in the subsection "brown mathematics" (26; xiii).

* Eadweard's description of his project in "Panorama of San Francisco" is quoted in Paul Hill's *Eadweard Muybridge* (New York: Phaidon, 2001. 60).

* Tutorow's *Stanford: Man of Many Careers* (Menlo Park (Calif): Pacific Coast, 1971) proved invaluable while researching for "Album 1: Palo Alto." The rules of the farm, slightly altered for my introduction of Stanford in the poem, are quoted in Tutorow's biography (165).

*Several lines from Rebecca Solnit's *River of Shadows: Eadweard Muybridge and the Technological Wild West* (New York: Viking, 2003. 6–7) appear in part 8 of "Album 1: Palo Alto". Solnit's book came out when I was writing this one, but I haven't yet given it the attention it deserves, fearing that her critically-lauded musical accuracy would take over my own version of Eadweard's story.

*The italicized lines in section 10 of "Album 2: Proof" were attributed to Diane Arbus as part of an exhibition at the National Gallery of Canada ("Fairy-Tales for Grown-Ups." January, 2001).

*The "rights" Eadweard declares in his lawsuit against Stanford in part one of "Album 3: Three Countries" were described in *Nature* (Vol. XXV. April 27, 1882. 591).

* In "Album 4: Pennsylvania: Man Ascending an Incline", quotations in italics (that describe Muybridge's plates) are from the Dover edition of *Human and Animal Locomotion* (New York: Dover, 1979), and informed by the first edition held at the main branch of the New York City Public Library.

* The long quotation and the phrase "a complete wreck" in section 2 of "Boarding an Exit: 1906" are taken from *The Evening Daily News* (April 18, 1906. Verb tense changed). Other information about the earthquake was gleaned from articles in *The New York Times* (for April 19, 1906).

* *Occident. Lantern slide, Palo Alto* printed with permission of Kingston Museum and Heritage Service, Kingston Museum (UK).

* *Contemplation Rock, Glacier Point,* by Eadweard Muybridge printed with permission of Iris & B. Gerald Cantor Center for Visual Arts at Stanford University.

* *Volcan Quetzaltenangeo* [sic] printed with permission of Stanford University Libraries, Special Collections.

*Portrait of Muybridge printed with permission of the University Archives and Records Center, University of Pennsylvania.

Every reasonable effort has been made to credit and contact the holders of copyright for materials significantly represented in this work. Nightwood Editions will gladly receive information allowing us to rectify any errors or omissions in subsequent editions.

Acknowledgements

Selections from *Muybridge's Horse* won first prize for English Poetry in the 2003 CBC Literary Awards. My thanks go out to the judges—George Bowering, Dionne Brand and PK Page—for collectively choosing them. My thanks, too, to Jesse Stewart, whose original confidence in these poems was a catalyst for it becoming this book.

Some of these poems have appeared, in slightly different form, in the following publications: *Descant, EnRoute, Grain, The New Quarterly*, and *modomnoc.*

Thanks to staff at the New York Public Library, to the National Gallery of Canada in Ottawa (especially Documentation Officer Hazel M. Mackenzie), Alice Egbert, John Mustain and Mattie Taormina at Stanford University, Nancy Miller at U Penn, and to the folks at the Kingston Museum (UK; especially archivist Jill Lamb) for providing source material for and/or access to certain images.

Great thanks goes out to early, insightful readers of this manuscript, especially Ken Babstock, Gregor Campbell, Kristal Davis, Stephen Henighan, Matt Holmes, Deanna Kruger and Deb Kortleve.

Further thanks are extended to Arthur Motyer for his inspired readings and faith in my attempts to get the words right, and Janice Kulyk Keefer for allowing me the right spaces at the right times. Other teachers along the way have saved me from various disasters, showing me some of the right things to read, and pointing out, with poise, the wrong ways to proceed: many thanks are due especially to Jay Howden, Deborah Wills and Bob Hogg, and to Sackville photographer Thaddeus Holownia for introducing me to both darkrooms and my first views of Eadweard's plates.

For various forms of support given while this book took shape, I'm indebted to my family: Angela, John, Darrin, Lynda, and especially my parents Larry and Janelle.

Further thanks are due to my editor, Silas White—and all the staff at Nightwood—whose belief in the project made it happen. And to Carleton Wilson for his superlative cover design.

Finally, for putting up with my banter about nineteenth-century chemistry, for intense listening to terrible early drafts, and for her constant, partisan cheerleading, I can't articulate adequate thanks to my partner, Kristal: there aren't sufficiently convincing ways to thank you enough, love. This book is for you, and our Davis.

Rob Winger grew up in a tiny Ontario town, and has since lived in eastern Canada and Asia. His work has been published in literary journals across the country.

Currently at work on a doctoral degree in English and Cultural Studies, Winger lives with his family in Ottawa, where he skates to work each winter.